THE GIG IS **UP**

THE GIG IS **UP**

Thrive in the Gig Economy, Where Old Jobs Are Obsolete

and Freelancing Is the Future

By Airbnb Speaker

OLGA MIZRAHI

GREENLEAF
BOOK GROUP PRESS

This publication is designed to provide accurate and authoritative information in regard to the subject matter covered. It is sold with the understanding that the publisher and author are not engaged in rendering legal, accounting, or other professional services. If legal advice or other expert assistance is required, the services of a competent professional should be sought.

Published by Greenleaf Book Group Press
Austin, Texas
www.gbgpress.com

Distributed by Greenleaf Book Group

For ordering information or special discounts for bulk purchases, please contact Greenleaf Book Group at PO Box 91869, Austin, TX 78709, 512.891.6100.

Design and composition by Jamie Ponchak, ohso! design
Cover design by Jamie Ponchak, ohso! design

Cataloging-in-Publication data is available.

Print ISBN: 978-1-62634-493-8

eBook ISBN: 978-1-62634-494-5

Part of the Tree Neutral® program, which offsets the number of trees consumed in the production and printing of this book by taking proactive steps, such as planting trees in direct proportion to the number of trees used: www.treeneutral.com

TreeNeutral®

Printed in the United States of America on acid-free paper

18 19 20 21 22 23   10 9 8 7 6 5 4 3 2 1

First Edition

To the hardworking hustlers that aren't normally seen.
I see you, and, yes, you are invited to the company party.

Table of Contents

||||||||||||||||||||||||||||||||||||||||||||||||||||||||||||||||||||||

CHAPTER 9

CHAPTER 10

APPENDIX

CHAPTER 1 > Introduction and Overview

What is this "gig economy" I keep hearing about? Is it just Uber and Upwork, or is it all freelance jobs? What about the temp and contract workers out there? Even if hired offline, are they now giggers? The answer is "Yes!" to all the above. Yet there is still some understandable confusion about what the gig economy is.

gig e•con•o•my

noun

project-based or
on-demand services
that can be provided
by anyone

This is because the gig economy is very diverse: it can include temporary workers, contract workers, consultants, and freelance CEOs, as well as freelance workers, entrepreneurs, and solo-preneurs. The gig economy is an amazing force that normalizes all types of project and temporary work and changes the concept of the workplace for everyone in and out of it.

Have you ever heard of the parable of the frog slowly being boiled alive? To play along, first we have to agree that having a frog is better than Chick-fil-A. The parable starts by warning us that if you boil the water first and proceed to put the frog in, the frog (a.k.a your lunch) will jump out of the hot water. The solution: put the frog in

continued next page

cold water, then slowly boil it, and it won't even know until . . . delicious frog sandwich time! In this story, we are the frog, and we haven't really noticed that the gig economy has been slowly boiling up around us. Now the good news: unlike our favorite new parable, instead of us all being killed, we will be made aware of how to use this new working world order to our advantage.

It is no wonder that we all feel the perpetual white water of change all around us. There is no standing still in today's work environment. No matter how fast we paddle, the current of change will keep rushing past. Nothing is speeding up that change more than the technology in your phone. The year 2017 marked the 10th anniversary of Apple's iPhone. It's led to the smartphone revolution fueling the remarkable change of the workplace as we know it. I am no exception to the opportunity (and the anxiety!) that this change brings. So I wasn't entirely surprised when I started seeing an interesting trend start to swell all around the blog I write for small business owners: the meteoric rise of the freelance economy.

Growth of the smartphone and widespread Internet access

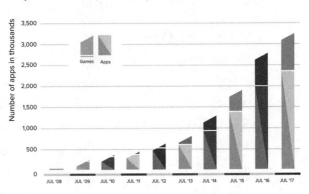

Number of available apps in the iTunes App Store from 2008 to 2017 (in 1,000s)

Today's workers are "digitally enabled" by having a computer in their pocket. When you consider that the first iPhone was released in 2007 with zero apps, the amount of growth in on-demand products and services since then is nothing short of staggering.

The ChunkOfChange.com blog is my labor of love; my day job is running a small creative agency in Long Beach, California, called ohso! design. When my business partner and I first started our e-commerce and graphic design company in 2004, we had a huge secret! Shhhhh! We could not disclose to potential clients that we had created an in-home studio, and like many, we set up a virtual "storefront." We masqueraded as an actual brick-and-mortar studio at a physical location and pretended that our scrappy team all actually went there to work every day. As freelance specialists worked on projects with us, they got ohso! design business cards and sometimes even (the drug dealer favorite) disposable cell phones with numbers that were their "business line." In reality, everyone preferred to work from home or the local coffee shop, and no one was the wiser as we churned out quality projects, ranging from slammin' websites to advertising campaigns to marketing strategy.

Why the deception? Because, as hard as it is to remember today, you really could not be taken seriously as a team if you didn't have people on a leash. As a leader, my ability to keep a project on track and produce stellar results was mistakenly equated with micromanaging the team from close quarters. If I had disclosed my hands-off approach to letting people do what they were awesome at, we wouldn't have won the projects that grew our budding company.

Even finding our freelance partners was an exercise in word-of-mouth and, sometimes, taking a chance on someone met through an online community.

Fast-forward, and gone are the days of the stereotypical on-demand worker.

Today's freelancers are *everywhere*–from Uber
drivers to high-powered corporate consultants.
No longer is there shame in having a "temporary"
job; all jobs are potentially temporary, it seems.
Now, you can find awesome people anytime,
anywhere, and anyhow.

A fundamental societal change—the removal of the shame in working flexibly, from anywhere, part time or full time, temp or permanently on demand—is what I believe is the fire stoking the engine of *independent work*.

As of 2017, WeWork became the third largest private start-up by market cap, behind Uber and Airbnb.[1] Worldwide, it manages 144 coworking spaces. What all three have in common is that they are gig economy energizers. WeWork is even changing the traditional concept of where large companies physically house their workers, recently reporting that big companies like Amazon, GE, and IBM are WeWork's largest growing segment. Just seven years ago, solo freelance workers used to dominate the cowork space's membership at 80%. As of this writing, independents now make up 40% of membership. Total membership is expected to more than double to 3.8 million by 2020, fueled by enterprise companies.

[1] Molla, R. (2017, August). "Uber Is the Most Valuable U.S. Startup, with Airbnb and WeWork Following Far Behind It." Recode. Retrieved from https://www.recode.net/2017/8/8/16113140/top-10-most-valuable-startups-uber-spacex-wework-airbnb

Let's take a further look together at the gig economy crystal ball and be amazed at where we've come in such a short timeline through a groundbreaking study that you'll see me refer to throughout this book.

The bulk of my statistics come from McKinsey Global Institute's 148-page report "Independent Work: Choice, Necessity, and the Gig Economy."[2] MGI surveyed roughly 8,000 respondents across Europe and the United States, asking about their income in the past 12 months—encompassing primary work and any other income-generating activities—and about their professional satisfaction and aspirations for work in the future.

MGI found that 20% to 30% of the working-age population in the US and the EU-15 (or up to 162 million individuals) engage in independent work and that 10% to 15% of the working-age population relies on independent work for their primary income. The study broke them down into four categories:

	Primary Income	Supplemental Income
Preferred Choice	Free Agents 30%	Casual Earners 40%
Out of Necessity	Reluctants 14%	Financially Strapped 16%

² McKinsey Global Institute. (2016, October). "Independent Work: Choice, Necessity, and the Gig Economy." Retrieved from http://www.mckinsey.com/global-themes/employment-and-growth/independent-work-choice-necessity-and-the-gig-economy

The numbers are growing, year over year. MGI sees "significant growth potential in the years ahead, based on the stated aspirations of individuals and growing demand for services from consumers and organizations alike."

MGI also found that, "while many independent workers want traditional jobs, roughly one in six people in traditional jobs would like to become a primary independent earner. In fact, for every primary independent worker who would prefer a traditional job, more than two traditional workers hope to shift in the opposite direction."

Survey results indicate that "the independent workforce could grow from around 27% of the US working-age population today to as much as 30% to 50% in the future."

Contrary to popular belief, independent work is not dominated by millennials; in fact, they represent less than one-quarter of independent workers. In the United States, the average age of digitally enabled independent workers is roughly 40. In actuality, "the independent workforce by and large resembles the traditional workforce. Independent earners come in all ages, education levels, incomes, and occupations."

Overall, the outlook for the gig economy is good. According to the study "Freelancing in America: 2016" conducted by the Freelancers Union and Upwork,[3] "freelancers say perceptions of freelancing are becoming more positive (63%) and respected as a career path (60%). Nearly half of full-time freelancers (46%) raised their rates in the past year, and more than half (54%) plan to raise them next year."

---

[3] Freelancers Union & Upwork. (2016, October). *Freelancing In America: 2016*. Retrieved from https://fu-prod-storage.s3.amazonaws.com/content/None/FreelancinginAmerica2016report.pdf

Of course there are challenges, too: lack of stability (i.e. unpredictable income), negotiation for fair wages, and access to health insurance and other benefits. Even so, it seems that the pros outweigh the cons.

According to the Freelancers Union study, "the majority of freelancers say that a diversified portfolio of clients is more stable than having one employer." Other benefits include feeling more respected, engaged, and empowered, as well as having freedom and flexibility.

In this book, we'll take a curated view of the gig economy and what it means for you specifically.

Here's a quick breakdown of content.

CHAPTER 1 - Introduction & Overview

CHAPTER 2 - All About Peer-to-Peer Platforms: What apps and sites are out there and how do they work?

CHAPTER 3 - Becoming a Freelance Elite: How to use Unique Value Proposition and your "-EST" to stand out from the crowd.

CHAPTER 4 - Slave to the App: The pros and cons of freelancing apps and online platforms and how to live with and without them.

CHAPTER 5 - The Things You're Not Going to Think About

CHAPTER 6 - Why Choose You?: The ins and outs of adding value to your work and how to reach the elusive "next level."

CHAPTER 7 - The Tipping Point: How to go from party of one to small business owner in the gig economy.

Throughout this book, in addition to all the killer stats, you'll see special "Spotlight" sections from real people living the gig life. You'll also hear many of the struggles endured, firsthand, by my token freelancer, Emma, in her words. Further, look for "Do This, Not That" tips toward the end of most chapters. Finally, many external resources referenced are gathered for you, dear reader, at chunkofchange.com/gigisup.

I look forward to being your trusty guide and getting us all paddling in the shifting white water ahead. As constant change is our only known, let's keep in touch as we go along this journey!

Let's continue the conversation:

🔗 linkedin.com/in/olgamizrahi
🐦 @olgamizrahi
📷 @chunkofchange

MAKING THE MOST OF

Peer-to-Peer Platforms

CHAPTER 2

In November 2016 I spoke at Airbnb's global conference to fellow Airbnb Superhosts on how to make their home listing stand out. Airbnb unveiled a new product, Trips, and I proceeded to become an "experience host."

Chairman of the SUP Board
Long Beach - SoCal on the Water
with a Business Marketing Expert

Wellness Experience
Hosted by Olga & Geoff

⏱ 2.5 hours total

🥤 1 snack, drinks and equipment

💬 Offered in English

💎 This is a crowd favorite. Olga & Geoff's experience is usually booked.

About your host Featured in Forbes and Fast Company, Olga Mizrahi is not just a hot #1 Business Author and Airbnb Speaker; She also helped launch Standup for the Cure, which raised over 600K to fight breast cancer.

What we'll do Mix pleasure (SUP - Standup Paddling) with business (Chat about business ideas, strategy or marketing). I've been giving access to the beautiful waters around my home, while consulting with my clients... + More

$89 per person
★★★★★ 4 reviews

See dates

f 🐦 ✉ ⑦ •••   Save to Wish List ♡

I take interested folks paddleboarding in the Pacific waters by my home while consulting about their marketing.

Los Angeles is Airbnb's largest "experience" market, and anyone can become one of these hosts to in-town visitors, mainly based on their skill and giving access to their passions. What kick-ass experience would you share with friendly people that came to you? That's right, you can now get paid for a passion as a fun side gig, regardless of what your career is.

According to *Forbes*, there were 53 million freelancers in America in 2016.[4]

By the year 2020, it is estimated that 50% of the US workforce will be working independently.

Thus, whether they're earning a living wage or bringing in extra money on the side, one of every two workers will be a "freelancer" in some capacity.

The Financial Times gives a similar diagnosis: "In today's gig economy . . . technology has cast a wider net, drawing in people who would not otherwise be gigging at all. Think of the retired person who occasionally lets out a spare room on Airbnb, or the office worker who picks up an extra passenger on the morning commute by using a ride-hailing app . . . The line between gigs and work is getting increasingly blurred."[5]

And the numbers are growing ever larger. MGI states that "research from Intuit projects that on-demand work will post more than 18 percent annual growth in the coming years, increasing the number of workers participating in on-demand platforms from 3.2 million to 7.6 million."[6]

The goal of this book is to help those of us firmly planted in freelance-land and also those new to the gig economy navigate this new economy from top to bottom. There's no better place to start than a look at the ever-growing digital platforms making it a reality.

[4] Rashid, B. (2016, Jan. 26). "The Rise of the Freelancer Economy." *Forbes*. Retrieved from http://www.forbes.com/sites/brianrashid/2016/01/26/the-rise-of-the-freelancer-economy/#46411069379a.
[5] Hook, L. (2015, December 29). "Year in a Word: Gig Economy." *Financial Times*. Retrieved from http://www.ft.com/cms/s/0/b5a2b122-a41b-11e5-8218-6b8ff73aae15.html.
[6] McKinsey Global Institute. (2016, October). "Independent Work: Choice, Necessity, and the Gig Economy." Retrieved from http://www.mckinsey.com/global-themes/employment-and-growth/independent-work-choice-necessity-and-the-gig-economy

It seems that many of us giggers are still in the dark about our online options. "MGI's own survey indicates that 30 percent of working-age Americans are not aware that they can use digital platforms to earn money. It seems likely that many people who could benefit from additional options for earning income and would choose to pursue this option simply do not yet know this avenue is open to them."

⊘ airbnb	**《Care.com**	**ᗡᗡ DOORDASH**
List, find, and rent vacation homes. Become an "experience host."	Find nannies, babysitters, & more.	Order on-demand food delivery from your favorite local restaurants.
DogVacay	**fiverr®**	**🏹 freelancer**
Pick a local dog lover to care for your pup.	Find professional services, in over 120 categories.	Find and hire professionals.
🐕 guru	**handy**	**listia**
Find and hire talented freelancers.	Book trusted home cleaners and handymen.	Trade goods without using money.
lyft	**𝓟 POSHMARK**	**POSTMATES**
Get taxi-like service or carpool locally.	Buy and sell fashion.	Get delivery from any store or restaurant in your city.

sittercity	SKILLSHARE	TaskRabbit
Find babysitters and nannies.	Take or teach online classes.	Hire pro taskers in your neighborhood.
✈ Thumbtack	**UBER**	Upwork™
Accomplish your personal projects.	Get a ride from a local driver.	Find freelancers to do anything that can be done on a computer.
urbansitter	workmarket	**Zaarly**
Find babysitters and nannies.	Use an on-demand workforce management system.	Hire local, hand-picked home services.

So, to start, here's a (non-exhaustive) laundry list of popular active platforms that allow you to connect with goods and services provided by other human beings.

There are a lot of options—too many to ignore, in fact. The trend of low-overhead, app-based startups appearing out of nowhere to lay siege to traditional businesses has become so widespread that it now has its own term: "Uber syndrome."[7]

In fact, MGI points out that career networking site "LinkedIn has seen the number of independent workers on its platform grow more than 40 percent in the past five years, a trend that spurred the creation of a dedicated platform for these workers, ProFinder."[8]

[7] Bernhard, K. (2015, November 3). "Why Uber Keeps Global C-Suites Up at Night." *Upstart Business Journal*. http://upstart. bizjournals.com/companies/startups/2015/11/03/why-uber-keeps-global-c-suites-up-at-night.html?ana=twt
[8] McKinsey Global Institute. (2016, October). "Independent Work: Choice, Necessity, and the Gig Economy." Retrieved from http://www.mckinsey.com/global-themes/employment-and-growth/independent-work-choice-necessity-and-the-gig-economy

These sites and apps have become a gateway to the freelance world, rapidly turning consumers into contractors. Of course, this gradual shift toward the gig economy has been happening for decades. In the rather bleak outlook that Stephen Hill describes in *Raw Deal: How the "Uber Economy" and Runaway Capitalism Are Screwing the American Worker*,[9] the increasing reliance of industry on 1099 workers (as a way to avoid paying for an employee safety net) has long been forcing people into unconventional roles. The digital platforms that utilize independent contractors on a wide scale are only accelerating that phenomenon.

Rather than lamenting that contracting is "the end of a good living," it's my plan to show you how digital marketplaces can make up a comfortable living, create an added cushion, offer a "next step," enable a flexible lifestyle (well-suited to multi-generational caretaking), or provide anything in between.

Consider how jobs used to work. Back in the day, looking for work meant calling up your employed friend Mike who'd heard there were openings down in the mail room. You'd work there for a handful of years before being noticed by Bob in Finance, who would promote you to office aide. Eventually, Manager Bill would notice how organized things had become in Finance and ask you to be his assistant, then later a community liaison, and before you'd know it, you'd be managing your own department.

Fast-forward to 2018. You call up your employed friend Mike, but he's now handling the work of Bob and Bill because the company downsized most of the Finance Department during the recession and never brought those jobs back. Mike's pretty sure they're not hiring, but he gives you the website application, which resembles a mid-'90s GeoCities page. Determined, you copy-paste your resume into the form to apply, only to discover that the submit button is unresponsive and their phones are answered by robots. It takes

[9] Hill, S. (2015). *Raw Deal: How the "Uber Economy" and Runaway Capitalism are Screwing the American Worker.* New York: St. Martin's Press.

some digging to discover that there is still a mail room, but its staff is subcontracted through an unrelated company in the Philippines. "Sorry, man. Have you tried LinkedIn?" Mike shrugs.

Needless to say, job hunting today is complicated. Most would agree that the hardest part of finding work in the new economy is just getting a foot in the door. Now, with so much digital infrastructure separating an employer and its applicants, you have no idea whether you're competing with ten people or ten thousand.

When you need money now, that level of uncertainty can easily turn into desperation, making it even harder to display that critical air of normalcy when you do manage to make the interview. What if there were a way to make money while job hunting and get that lucky foot in the door? Well, that's the modern fantasy that peer-to-peer platforms are trying to fulfill.

People have always taken odd jobs when times got tough, be it watching a neighbor's kids or driving a friend's mom to the doctor. In that regard, the emergence of digital marketplaces (like TaskRabbit) isn't so much a revolution of the sharing economy as it is us rediscovering our local handyman. Even so, the Yellow Pages could never give the local handyman instant access to millions of people with a squeaky door—the way Thumbtack can.

A nanny looking for a new position may still find leads by talking to families on the playground, but she could also make herself available to "more than 20 million members in 18 countries" by posting a profile on Care.com.

The real selling point for these platforms is their low barrier to entry: UrbanSitter will let your babysitter profile go live with either a subscription fee or upon submission of an introduction video, while a new Upwork freelancer can start applying for jobs in as little as 24 hours. Even if you're still holding out for a salaried position,

Surprisingly, these platforms are still considered in their infancy. According to MGI, "Despite their extensive media coverage, digital 'on-demand' or 'sharing economy' platforms such as Uber, Lyft, TaskRabbit, Upwork, Freelancer.com, Thumbtack, Airbnb, and the like facilitate only a small fraction of independent work today. . . . [O]nly about 4 percent of the working-age population has used digital platforms to generate income."[10] Those numbers are growing every day, though.

services like these can help individuals bring in funds while maneuvering the job market, providing a cushion that can make a difference.

Capitalism is all about pulling yourself up by your bootstraps and making it work. It just so happens that these platforms are an easy way to get started. So let's start by getting to know them and what benefits they offer their users.

The Pros: Safety in Numbers

As services created by and for the digital revolution, peer-to-peer platforms offer a level of built-in security for the beginning entrepreneur that you won't find in the go-it-alone model.

[10] McKinsey Global Institute. (2016, October). "Independent Work: Choice, Necessity, and the Gig Economy." Retrieved from http://www.mckinsey.com/global-themes/employment-and-growth/independent-work-choice-necessity-and -the-gig-economy

Although you might meet a potential client at the library who's willing to pay you $25 per hour to edit her novel, if you finish the job and she decides she doesn't feel like paying, there's nothing short of the small claims court system that can convince her otherwise. Fickle clients are a minefield for the inexperienced freelancer, and the stress of not being paid is sometimes more painful than not being able to find work at all.

In that regard, the assurances of a third-party system sound like a dream. For instance, if a TaskRabbit tasker shows up and completes their task, they submit their invoice through the TaskRabbit system, which then automatically bills the client who booked the task. If there's trouble processing the payment, that's TaskRabbit's problem—not the tasker's. In order to preserve their reputation and keep that tasker active, TaskRabbit will resolve the issue and see that the money changes hands one way or another, allowing the tasker to keep working, confident in the knowledge that they're not the one who has to start dialing lawyers.

The struggle is real:

In Southern California, I'm an Airbnb experience host, but in Northern California, I have a place in the mountains listed on Airbnb. As an Airbnb Superhost, I had an experience where a language barrier caused renter Pedro to ask "split it?" regarding a site-required fee. I told Pedro that the funds go to the site, not me, so there is no way to "split it" with me. It turned out Airbnb was monitoring the conversation and called me (seemingly out of nowhere) as a result of this exchange. They explained that Pedro was confused, and so, if I accepted his half fee, Airbnb would gladly pony up the rest.

There's also some modicum of physical safety offered with this model. For the platforms that track your geolocation, the likelihood that a client-turned-mugger could pretend they had nothing to do with your injuries the day they hired you is minimized. The fact that women make up 18.9% of drivers on ridesharing platforms[11] (compared to composing exactly 1% of cab drivers for the whole of New York City[12]) shows that apps are addressing concerns that may keep women away from the traditional cabbie model.

There seem to be a lot of taskers who have taken jobs through the service that they never would have otherwise picked up in another setting. "I sat by an elevator on Halloween as a bouncer for a drag party," says TaskRabbiter Emma. "It was dark, the elevator door was literally in an alley, and I was in pretty scandalous boots. I was making $20 an hour, and figured that, if anything weird happened, TaskRabbit would probably cover it."

The Cons: The Dead End

Dead-end jobs have never been good news. The danger of becoming dependent on a job without security or benefits, that's your mother's worst nightmare. Although convenience apps are currently taking the world by storm, it's important to recognize that just being iOS-optimized doesn't make something revolutionary.

Unless you're hoping to run a hotel someday, learning how to be the best Airbnb host probably isn't going to help you achieve your dreams.

[11] SherpaShare. (2015, October 23). "The Top Demographic Trends of the On-Demand Workforce." Retrieved from https://sherpashare.com/share/the-top-demographic-trends-of-the-on-demand-workforce/.
[12] Gardner, R. (2014, February 10). "New York's Female Cabbies and How They Drive." *The Wall Street Journal*. Retrieved from http://www.wsj.com/articles/SB10001424052702304104504579375102464407142

In her time undercover in the gig economy, *Fast Company* journalist Sarah Kessler said of her very brief Postmates experience: "If you work for Postmates and you don't beat your coworker to accept deliveries that might fill your shift, you—not Postmates—are out of luck. If you get a flat tire, you—not Postmates—are out of luck. And if there aren't enough jobs to go around, you— not Postmates—are out of luck."[13]

There is simplicity in tasks that don't require much skill—like picking up Chinese food, a popular Postmates request. Depending on where you are, the demand might be enough to provide a stable income (minus the cost of gas and vehicle maintenance).

Even so, convenience apps provide little in the way of learning experiences to justify the risks. If a job is less than a few years from being replaced by a robot, it's generally not a good idea to get too attached.

[13] Kessler, S. (2014, March 18). "Pixel and Dimed: On (Not) Getting By in the Sharing Economy." *Fast Company*. Retrieved from http://www.fastcompany.com/3027355/pixel-and-dimed-on-not-getting-by-in-the-gig-economy.

The Breakdown

It would be impossible to describe each and every peer-to-peer platform that's cropped up in the past few years. I imagine this bodes well for the free market, seeing as smaller services are going to be competing with one another to attract the best talent, but the amount of options can be overwhelming.

In this section, I roll up the most promising platforms in four categories:

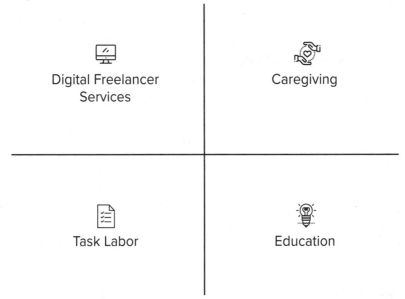

Digital Freelancer Services

Caregiving

Task Labor

Education

In true capitalist fashion, Upwork is already eating its competition. The Upwork (oDesk-Elance) merger from April 2015 is projected to earn the conglomerate more than $10 billion in revenue by 2021.[14]

I've broken down the services by the types of work they provide and, in order to keep this section short, have only profiled the biggest competitor in each.

---

[14] Pofeldt, E. (2015, May 5). "Elance-oDesk Becomes 'Upwork' In Push To Build $10B In Freelancer Revenues." *Forbes.* Retrieved from http://www.forbes.com/sites/elainepofeldt/2015/05/05/elance-odesk-becomes-upwork-today-odesk-brand-gets-phased-out/.

Upwork
(Digital Services)

OVERVIEW:
A hiring platform geared toward connecting writers, designers, programmers, and artists to clients in need of their talents

IDEAL FREELANCER:
Liberal arts BA, computer literate, willing to work on tight deadlines

COMPETING PLATFORMS:
Fiverr, Freelancer.com, Guru, WorkMarket, Ziptask

|||||||||||||||||||||||||||||||||||||||||||||||||||||||||||||||||||||||||||||||||||||||||||||||||||||||||||||||||||||

PROS:
Average days to hire is 1–3, compared to a traditional hiring timeline of up to 43 days

Huge variety of job postings

Transparent two-way feedback process

CONS:
Upwork charges a 10% service fee from each transaction

Upwork's #1 client country by spending is the United States, while the #1 earning country is India. In other words, the struggle to compete against people who will work for $3 per hour is real

Care.com
(Caregiving)

OVERVIEW:
Marketplace for child care, adult and senior care, pet care, housekeeping, and related jobs

IDEAL FREELANCER:
Previous caregiving experience, people person, friendly and punctual, with a mode of transportation

COMPETING PLATFORMS:
DogVacay, SitterCity, UrbanSitter

PROS:
Information is secure, as both caregivers and clients have to go through a number of stages of verification before contacting one another

Well-known, making for a densely populated marketplace

Households can set up payroll through Care.com, which will withhold tax for their caregiver; Care.com will even prepare and file the household employment tax returns for $200/quarter[15]

CONS:
Priority visibility given to caregivers who are paid premium subscribers, rather than the most qualified profiles

Applicants must pay before contacting caregivers

Average time to hire highly variable: securing employment for a new caregiver can take anywhere from days to months

---

[15] Care.com. (2015). Service FAQs. Retrieved from https://www.care.com/homepay/service-faqs-1402251530.

TaskRabbit
(Labor)

OVERVIEW:

An online and mobile marketplace that allows users to outsource minor jobs and tasks to others in their neighborhood. Users name the task they need done and the price they are willing to pay, and a network of preapproved contractors bid to complete the job

IDEAL FREELANCER:

Friendly, extroverted, knows their way around a toolbox

COMPETING PLATFORMS:

Handybook, Thumbtack, Zaarly

||||||||||||||||||||||||||||||||||||||||||||||||||||||||||||||||||||||||||||||||||||||||||||||||||||

PROS:

Plenty of work available for a variety of skill levels

Payments for tasks are processed within 1–2 business days

Easy cancellations

Taskers set their own hourly rate

CONS:

Only available in a handful of cities

TaskRabbit charges a 30% service fee, forcing taskers to charge higher rates

Taskers have to respond to tasks within 30 minutes or risk penalty, resulting in an always-on-call stress for the worker

Skillshare
(Education)

OVERVIEW:

Skillshare is an online learning community for creators. Teachers can host online classes, unaccredited, that students can pay to participate in. Popular categories include creative arts, design, lifestyle, technology, and entrepreneurship

IDEAL FREELANCER:

Highly experienced professional, well-organized, computer literate, with teaching instincts

COMPETING PLATFORMS:

Maven.co, Udemy, Verbling

PROS:

User-friendly tools for teachers and students

All teachers with a class of 25 students are entitled to monthly revenue

Bonuses for referrals

CONS:

Complex royalty system

Teachers have to invest in their own marketing efforts, as they compete for a small pool of active subscribers

Not enough students? No monthly payout. But you'll have to conduct the class regardless

It might seem unusual that education is on this list until you consider the data. FlexJobs, an online marketplace that connects freelancers and employers, tracked 50 industries hiring freelancers between December 1, 2015, and March 1, 2016. According to *Fast Company*, FlexJobs found that the following are the top 10 industries for freelancers are:[16]

1. Computer & IT
2. Administrative
3. Accounting & Finance
4. Customer Service
5. Software Development
6. Medical & Health
7. Project Management
8. Research Analyst
9. Writing
10. Education & Training

Among these industries, it seems that choice is the uniting factor. MGI notes that "those who find work through digital labor platforms (such as Upwork, Thumbtack, or Uber) represent a unique segment of the labor force. They are particularly likely to be independent by choice."

In the United States, 87 percent of 'digitally enabled' independent earners are gig workers by choice.[17]

#SideGigs

Recently Priceonomics data analysts looked at what side gig income tens of thousands of folks were earning when applying to college loan provider Earnest. The top money making platform, by a large margin, was Airbnb. So renting out your real estate is

[16] Lindzon, J. (2016, April 5). "The Top 10 Industries for Freelancers." *Fast Company*. Retrieved from https://www.fastcompany.com/3058559/the-future-of-work/the-top-10-industries-for-freelancers.
[17] McKinsey Global Institute. (2016, October). "Independent Work: Choice, Necessity, and the Gig Economy." Retrieved from http://www.mckinsey.com/global-themes/employment-and-growth/independent-work-choice-necessity-and-the-gig-economy

the top side gig money maker, with a $924/mo average. The rest of the apps don't paint such a rosy picture, with 84% of the loan applicants making under $500/mo from their side gigs.

How much do people make in the sharing economy?

AVERAGE AND MEDIAN MONTHLY INCOME PER SHARING ECONOMY WORKER

RANK	COMPANY	AVERAGE/MO	MEDIAN/MO
1	Airbnb	$924	$440
2	TaskRabbit	$380	$110
3	Lyft	$377	$210
4	Uber	$364	$155
5	Doordash	$229	$100
6	Postmates	$174	$70
7	Etsy	$151	$40
8	Fiverr	$98	$60
9	Getaround	$98	$70
	OVERALL	**$299**	**$109**

Whether by choice or necessity, it's rare to be able to make a decent living while a third-party takes commission off the top, so don't sign up for any of these expecting to quit your day job. Not yet, at least.

That being said, the ease of entry into these services makes these a good jumping-off point for the beginning freelancer. Whether or not you plan on being self-employed, it's hard to deny the benefit of exploring potential passions.

For now, just keep in mind time is money. So be sure to spend that time on activities that will lead somewhere in the long run.

Data is based on tens of thousands of Earnest loan applicants.
Source: https://priceonomics.com/how-much-are-people-making-from-the-sharing/

Greetings from Emma, your token freelancer. These are her words:

I stumbled headfirst into the freelance lifestyle. After being called a "contractor" for a year at a company that had no intention of actually hiring me, I found myself on Craigslist in search of a way to make ends meet. Along came Postmates, which claimed I could make as much as $1,000 a week just picking up groceries for people around town. After passing the instant background check, I took an unpaid day from work to go to the orientation, where I enthusiastically asked questions about user demographics, average payout, and how soon I could start. Alas, it was only a week before I was informed that, of the thirty people they had crammed into the orientation chamber, I had not been selected to be a member of the Orange County fleet. Better luck next time.

My unhappy contract continued a few months longer. During that time, I came across an article about how digital freelance services were making it easier than ever to leave terrible jobs. Links from that article brought me to Upwork (where I could, apparently, use my English degree to edit papers for $20 an hour). I signed up instantly. Upwork approved my profile within 24 hours.

Upwork ended up coming in handy. My first month on board was the hardest I've ever worked in my life. I edited papers for pennies, but the bills got paid.

Soon after, I signed up and was approved to be a TaskRabbit tasker. I had never been so desperate for a paycheck. For the next few months, it was a blur of piecemeal jobs, editing assignments, and sleepless nights. And it was just the beginning.

~ Emma, The Eccentric Assistant

Spotlight:
Growing Up with the Internet

Emma isn't just a case study. She came to me, through TaskRabbit, as a personal assistant. We worked together for about a year until she moved on to bigger and better things as a Fulbright Scholar.

Finding help online isn't a new thing for me. In my day job, for years, I've searched out talented freelancers on the Web. Emma wasn't the first and won't be the last either. At this point, ohso! design might as well be a virtual global office, considering all my workers are scattered across the world. One of ohso!'s interns even reached out to me through Facebook, of all places, and he ended up being an incredible social media guru.

DO **THIS** / NOT **THAT**

Do:: Familiarize yourself with the popular peer-to-peer marketplaces and take advantage of free trials and discounts for signing up to get a taste for the system.

There's nothing stopping you from downloading Uber, TaskRabbit, Postmates, or any of the other platforms mentioned here on your smartphone. With convenience services becoming more a part of our daily lives, it pays to get a personal look at what they're doing well (and what they're not).

Whether you're an employer (who's been putting off errands) or a potential freelancer (wondering what it would be like to work for a service), nearly all of these platforms offer some kind of new member discount. Hire a tasker/driver/sitter and ask about their experience, then decide for yourself how you want to participate in the future.

Don't: Blindly sign up for a bunch of services and try to tackle it all at once.

You can't do it all. Even if you're pretty sure you can deliver Barbara's dry cleaning, chauffeur Alice to bingo, babysit Sam, and write a press release for Bobby on Wednesday, you probably can't cram it all in. Start slowly and build your network skillfully . . . or suffer the wrath of bad reviews.

I consider this growing digitalization of the freelance world a trend that is close to my heart. Even though I'm not a "digital native," I was an early immigrant. It was the late '90s when I fell in love with the World Wide Web, back when everyone still thought Ask Jeeves was going to outlast Google. There are things I used to dedicate hours to doing that, now, my dog accidentally does when he sits on my iPhone. So getting to the point that the Internet has become such an integral part of not only our social life but our employability—that's a pretty exciting trend, in my book.

As one of the early adopters of the Internet (as well as someone who has been a part of the "freelance economy" before they even knew what to call it), I feel that it's my responsibility to guide others through this change intelligently. I want people to avoid thinking that it's "workocalypse" (the way some books would have you believe). Instead, it's merely the inevitable way that things are headed.

This book isn't just intended to help you survive. It's designed to help you thrive in the new economy.

Showcasing You at Your Best

Now that you're familiar with gigging sites and apps—your gateway to the freelance economy—it's time to learn what it takes to put your unique skills on the market.

First, how do you know you're part of the gig economy? Well, you probably fit into one (or more) of these categories:

A. You have a day job, but you're not sure how much longer it will last

B. You work for an employer by day and have moonlighting gigs on the side

C. You get paid (by a business or individual), but tax is not deducted from your gross payment

D. You earn money from various sources on a project-by-project basis

E. You cannot currently claim anyone as an "employer"

According to an independent study commissioned by Freelancers Union and ELance-oDesk,[18] there are five main categories of freelancers:

Independent Contractors	Moonlighters
(40% OF FREELANCERS)	**(27% OF FREELANCERS)**
No employer, and do freelance, temporary, or supplemental work on a project-by-project basis	Professionals with a primary, traditional job who also moonlight doing freelance work

Diversified Workers	Temporary Workers	Business Owners Who Consider Themselves Freelancers
(18% OF FREELANCERS)	**(10% OF FREELANCERS)**	**(5% OF FREELANCERS)**
Multiple sources of income; mix of traditional and freelance work	Single employer, client, job, or contract project, where employment is temporary	Business owners with 1–5 employees

[18] Freelancer: Union & Elance-oDesk, (2014). *Freelancing in America: A National Survey of the New Workforce*, 5–6

The secure jobs of the last century are disappearing, which means that, sooner or later, most people are going to have to learn how to be their own bosses.

Understanding the mindset of an entrepreneur will give you the tools you need to grapple with instability, no matter how or when it sneaks up on you.

First, let's think about what it really means to be a freelancer.

Merriam-Webster defines "freelance" as follows: *1) a person who acts independently without being affiliated with or authorized by an organization; 2) a person who pursues a profession without a long-term commitment to any one employer*[19]

Perhaps, in 25 years, the words "profession" and "career" will be antiquated. Merriam-Webster calls a career "a profession for which one trains and which is undertaken as a permanent calling." Does that even happen anymore?

I don't think I know anyone with a "career" these days. I know people with jobs and gigs and talents, but I doubt any of my colleagues consider what they do to earn an income today their "life's work" or "permanent calling." That's pretty intense. And, even if you wanted to, it's almost impossible to find the same employer willing to sign your paycheck until you retire.

[19] Merriam Webster Online Dictionary, 2017. "Freelance." Retrieved from http://www.merriam-webster.com/dictionary/freelance

Perhaps the more relevant question here is: if "career" doesn't mean the same thing that it used to, what does it mean now?

Well, when my generation (i.e. Gen Xers and, even previously, baby boomers) grew up, there was a distinct career path, based on technical training, provided by an institution. A career wasn't necessarily synonymous with a "calling" or passion. It was simply what you chose, in life, to do. It was a product of industrialization.

Now, however, we have the maker movement and apprenticeships and paid internships. Brought forth by need or necessity, the newer generation explores a wide variety of things more actively and seeks out the kinds of jobs and tasks they enjoy doing. I think, today, if someone thinks about what their life's calling is, it looks drastically different than it used to. It's about satisfaction, not security. You can thank the Internet and technology for this seismic shift.

Luckily, it's entirely possible to make a career out of freelancing. It's one thing to make a living doing odd jobs—but if you're climbing up a professional ladder of your own design, where each job is a wrung that's either going to hoist you up or send the whole thing crashing down, that's another thing entirely. A good freelancer takes a page from the entrepreneurial atlas. She isn't lost in the sea of instability, waiting for the U.S.S. Corporate to throw her a raft. The best freelancer grabs some driftwood, picks a direction, and starts kicking.

So how do you pick a direction? First, let's talk about how people pick you.

Use Your Secret Weapon:
Unique Value Proposition

IIIIIIIIIIIIIIIIIIIIIIIIIIIIIIIIIIIIIIIIIIIIIIIIIIIIIIIIIIIIIIIIIIIIIIIIIIII

In my last book, *Sell Local, Think Global*, I tasked small business owners with finding their Unique Value Proposition (UVP).[20] It's a concept I originally developed to help businesses discover the message they want to send their customers.

What most don't realize, though, is that going freelance makes you a business of one: you become the marketing director, PR representative, accounting lead, research team, and project manager of You, Inc.

Therefore, you need to ask yourself the number one question that matters: Why choose you?

To answer this incredibly difficult question, you must put yourself in the shoes of those doing the choosing and understand what unique skills and value you bring to the table that makes you irresistible. In terms of strengths, timing, location, and, sometimes, pure dumb luck, what makes you the BEST choice? What are you willing to do that others cannot or are unwilling to? That is where UVP comes in as a tool.

It's not about simply figuring out how to portray yourself to the outside world; it's about pinpointing what makes you different enough and then carrying that message around boldly, wherever you go.

---

[20] Mizrahi, O. (2014). "Chapter 1: Change Your Message." In *Sell Local, Think Global: 50 Innovative Ways to Make a Chunk of Change and Grow Your Business*. Pompton Plains, NJ: Career Press 17–40.

See, a value proposition is an inherent promise of benefit. It is usually measured in terms of "benefit minus cost." A large part of determining value lies in comparing the alternatives.

A Unique Value Proposition, on the other hand, communicates the special contribution you are able to provide to the market in a way that is markedly different from your competitors. A solid UVP is:

A statement that outlines why you belong in the competitive marketplace	A directive to convey to yourself and potential clients	A different message that is unique to you and you alone	An explanation about why you truly stand apart

The bottom line is that if you can clearly communicate your difference, then there will be some sort of impression formed in the mind of the person doing the choosing. If you can't communicate a distinct difference, something worse happens: there's no impression formed. You're ignored; you're an afterthought. In other words: differentiate or die.

Think of your own behavior when Googling a question. If you click through on a top result and it doesn't make sense, what is the first thing you do? You click the back button and return to the search results. "Ignore" is the first response, not "why don't I contact this web page and see what they really mean?"

Do I Need a UVP When I'm Just Starting Out?

Imagine if Apple announced it was going to be #1 in hardware, athletic shoes, and solar energy by next year. You'd call them crazy. Even with all the money and resources at their disposal, Apple couldn't possibly connect to all three of those markets simultaneously and would burn through a ton of dough trying to do it.

That's exactly the mistake most freelancers make when they first start working for themselves: they take on any project that will pay, regardless of how those jobs fit together, and blame themselves when they eventually drop the ball on (at least) one of them.

Take the time to narrow your focus, craft a concrete UVP, and integrate it into your professional life. Remember, UVP doesn't stop with your job title. There are plenty of editors, programmers, artists, you-name-its on the market. So why should someone choose you over that other guy? The freelance economy is saturating the market with contractors—whether you're on TaskRabbit or off the grid—which creates a lot of noise you need to cut through when getting started.

With freelance competition increasing, it's no longer about the -ers: being better, faster, cheaper. It's about the -ests, your "bests": what you bring to the table that stops clients from ever considering another offer. The -est is what separates the struggling freelancer from what I call the Freelance Elite.

What's Your -EST?

Defining that special something you're good at, the core qualities that really capture why someone should choose you, depends on what you already know how to do. Here's just a handful of ideas to help you zero in on an effective -est.

What you have to offer depends, of course, on how you plan on marketing your skills. Do you sell products (Etsy, eBay, PayPal)? Or do you provide a service (plumbing, writing, cooking)? Figure out which of these descriptions most applies to you and your work.

-est don't be an er

You might distinguish yourself through "product power" because your work has

- ☑ high perceived value (i.e. the buyer is pleasantly surprised by the price of your product);
- ☑ unique packaging;
- ☑ standout design;
- ☑ ease of use;
- ☑ a unique solution;
- ☑ superior performance over competing products.

Or, you might differentiate yourself because of your "service power" by offering

- ☑ faster response time;
- ☑ the ability to offer more for less money;
- ☑ a high level of expertise;
- ☑ an excellent industry reputation;
- ☑ the perception that you bring more to the table (i.e. an intangible);
- ☑ availability of service at a particular time of need.

Even on peer-to-peer platforms (like TaskRabbit), the most successful workers are the ones who have learned to narrow their focus and build a steady client base. Long story short, "pick yourself." Rise to the top of the pool by figuring out what you're good at and committing to be the best at it.

Pick Yourself

Authority?

You want the authority to create, to be noticed and to make a difference? You're waiting for permission to stand up and speak up and ship?

Sorry. There's no authority left.

Oprah has left the building. She can't choose you to be on her show because her show is gone. YouTube wants you to have your own show now, but they're not going to call you.

Dick Clark has left the building. He's not going to be able to get you a record deal or a TV gig because his show is long gone. iTunes and a hundred other outlets want you to have your own gig now, but they're not going to call you either.

Neither is Rodney Dangerfield or the head of programming at Comedy Central. Louis CK has famously proven that he doesn't need to the tyranny of the booker—he picked himself.

Our cultural instinct to wait to get picked. To seek out the permission, authority and safety that comes from a publisher or talk show host or even a blogger saying, "I pick you."

Once you reject that impulse and realize that no one is going to select you—that Prince Charming has chosen another house—then you can actually get to work.

The myth that the CEO is going to discover you and nurture you and ask you to join her for lunch is just that, a Hollywood myth.

Once you understand that there are problems just waiting to be solved, once you realize that you have all the tools and all the permission you need, then opportunities to contribute abound. Not the opportunity to have your resume picked from the pile, but the opportunity to lead.

When we take responsibility and eagerly give credit, doors open. When we grab a microphone and speak up, we're a step closer to doing the work we're able to do.

Most of all, when you buckle down, confront the lizard and ship your best work, you're becoming the artist that you are capable of becoming.

No one is going to pick you. Pick yourself.

PICK YOURSELF BY SETH GODIN. I KEEP THIS SIGNED COPY IN MY OFFICE TO REMIND MYSELF OF THESE TRUTHS, EVERYDAY.

If you want more help figuring out your UVP, head over to ChunkofChange.com/gigisup and download the full-sized UVP worksheet. It's free. Promise. Can't wait? You can always do the smaller version in the Appendix.

Communicating Your UVP

||||||||||||||||||||||||||||||||||||||||||||||||||||||||||||||||||||||

The things that make you awesome, those UVP points, are features of you. What the person that chooses you wants to understand is how that will benefit them.

Please take a moment right now to fill in the blanks to this game changer:

I'm awesome because

_____

and that benefits you by

_____

Think of the last tech product that you tried to shop for. Did your eyes glaze over when reading the gazillion features? Two point three-six million-dot LCD with built-in 400 Mbps Ethernet . . . that meant absolutely nothing to you? How is that experience different from when a review tells you about an amazing tech product? "OMG this thing takes amazing pictures. It captured my squirmy toddler smiling with no blur!"

Spotlight: Liya the Consultant

In 2009, NPR hosted a podcast entitled "Piecing Together a Living in the Gig Economy." Back then, the term "gig economy" was synonymous with the financial crisis, wherein newly unemployed people would try to make a living by gigging (i.e. working as many part-time jobs as needed to make ends meet).[21]

One woman lamented the increasing instability in her work life, saying:

> "In the last two years, I've been a wedding singer; I'm a business consultant; I'm a copy editor; I do graphic designing for a Web site; I'm a family consultant; I teach parenting classes. And the other day . . . I started to tell someone what I did and I actually started to feel embarrassed."[22]

She wasn't alone. The rhetoric of "new independence," it seems, hadn't quite taken hold. Many of the guests on the podcast were worried about where they were going to end up next. Now, even though some of those displaced workers are back on their feet, it's typically not in the way they thought they would be.

---

[21] Hook, L. (2015, December 29). "Year in a Word: Gig Economy." *Financial Times*. Retrieved from http://www.ft.com/cms/s/0/b5a2b122-a41b-11e5-8218-6b8ff73aae15.html.
[22] Conan, N. (2009, April 2). "Piecing Together a Living in the 'Gig Economy.'" NPR. Retrieved from http://www.npr.org/templates/transcript/transcript.php?storyId=100249858.

The Gig is Up

This sounds just like Liya Swift. It'd be easy to mistake Liya for another millennial hipster: she sports black-framed glasses, a mauve turtleneck and scrunchy, and a smartphone. No one would guess that she's over thirty, much less old enough to be a former executive assistant for a company gutted by the 2008 housing bubble. Young and very suddenly unemployed, she could have moved back home and mourned her loss. But that's not Liya. She decided that she would work her way back to independence; after returning to school to study SEO marketing, she managed to rebrand herself in the new economy. Now, she's a project manager with plenty of irons in the fire, bringing in a healthy middle-class wage and enjoying her freedom.

"I really treasure my independence," Liya says. "I really treasure being able to go and do the laundry at 3:00 if I want to, or just run to the grocery store. I don't like feeling like I'm just in the same 9:00 to 5:00 humdrum world as everyone else."

While, like most freelancers, it's a challenge to describe everything she does on a day-to-day basis, she says her life now revolves around project demands for four main clients, involving anything from copywriting to social media.

"They say you create the position you want to have. With my main client—whom I've been with for four years now—I started out as a copywriter for them, then I moved into an SEO role for them. I still do SEO for them, but now I've had to start using what I learned in school as an English major—I lean on that a great deal, because I'm editing content streams. I work with a number of writers, where I edit all their work and I give them their assignments, and make sure they turn it around in a week. That's just one client that I service."

For Liya, the forced career change turned out to be a blessing in disguise. Though she had often considered being self-employed, the trappings of her salary position had a way of keeping her in the lifestyle. Once that was gone, she realized that she had always been more suited for contracting.

"I'm project-oriented," Liya explains. "That's something I really figured out about myself when I was in project development, because we'd have a build and we'd work towards a completion date and that was very inspiring for me. Even if I wasn't all about building buildings, it was inspiring to know I was part of a team who were working towards achieving a goal. If you take me away from being able to work in that environment, I won't be happy. I know I need a goal."

Liya's project-oriented mindset was no doubt what helped her transition so easily from the salary world to freelancing. When forced to reset, rather than moving blindly into the first offer to present itself, Liya outlined the skills she needed to develop and set herself on a path to earn those skills. For her, that meant technical school, followed by an apprenticeship (which ended up being with her first client). Liya admits, however, that traditional school isn't necessarily the only way to reeducate yourself.

"Education can mean a bunch of different things. It depends on how you're wired: some people do fine learning sitting in a classroom listening to someone lecture, or they maybe need that experience to get an overview of what the actual field entails. . . . Education can also just be really applying yourself, and doing a lot of research and creating a program for yourself. You just have to be disciplined enough to do it."

Liya says the transition from traditional office life to freelancing can still be a struggle. When there are no set work hours, it's easy to fall into the habit of working all the time, at least mentally. "It's very hard to turn off. My mind is constantly working on other people's projects. I'm constantly thinking of ideas for what's going on with them. I miss being able to turn it off."

On the other hand, nothing can compare to the freedom working for yourself can bring.

"It can be very rewarding, because you might have that great idea at 2:00 in the morning. I always need to know I'm effecting a change in someone's life, or their narrative campaign, or some ultimate goal. When I'm in a system that takes that away from me and I don't get to see how I'm actually contributing to make something happen for them, it's discouraging. I had a sort of depression, a malaise would set in, when I was in the 9:00 to 5:00. I don't get that anymore."

[⇨ DO **THIS** / NOT **THAT** ⇦]

Do: Fill out the Unique Value Proposition worksheet fully.

There's no doubt about it. Crafting your UVP is a difficult process. But it's an essential one. Go to ChunkofChange.com/gigisup today and download the UVP worksheet. Take an hour or two and fill it out completely. Get a friend or colleague to help you expand your perspective. By the time you're done, you'll have a more complete picture of your offerings and be able to clearly answer the vital "why choose you" question.

Don't: Try to be all things to all people.

Another benefit of creating a thoroughly fleshed out UVP is that you'll start to develop a clearer picture of what you don't do and who you don't service. A big part of UVP is determining what you can offer that others are unable or unwilling to provide. During this process, it's important to figure those things out for yourself, too. I'm sure you've heard the phrase "jack of all trades, master of none." Nobody wants to be that guy. You need to be a master. So figure out where you're a rock star and stick with that angle.

CHAPTER 4

Don't Be a Slave to the App

Digital marketplaces are essential for transitioning into the freelance life: they're easy to access, are filled with built-in clientele, and put you just one email verification away from being your own boss. So what do you need the rest of this book for?

As I'm sure you've guessed by now, there's a big "HOWEVER" coming. Although I am usually the first to defend the merits of freelance apps, it's important for those wanting to make a real living to understand the danger of relying solely on one site as a means for putting food on the table. For every story of a TaskRabbit bringing home $7,000 a month,[23] there are thousands of others whose most profitable day—eight-and-a-half hours, without a lunch break—earned them just $95 . . . or roughly $11 per hour.[24]

As an aside, I should note that there are times that I'll never leave the app. I simply have no interest in taking an Uber outside of the platform (hello, uninsured creepy driver) or renting a guest house outside of Airbnb (hi there, broken furnace).

Indeed, the real danger of online marketplaces is in how easy it is to get trapped in the system. The successful ones are built in a way that gets you virtually addicted.

Upwork promises that freelancers with the highest "job success" score will be featured more often to employers, a factor influenced most heavily by the number of jobs they've completed through the site.

---

[23] Zimmerman, J. (2015, March 3). "Working for TaskRabbit" *Time*. Retrieved from http://time.com/money/3714829/working-for-taskrabbit/

[24] Kessler, S. (2014, March 18). "Pixel and Dimed: On (Not) Getting By in the Sharing Economy." *Fast Company*. Retrieved from http://www.fastcompany.com/3027355/pixel-and-dimed-on-not-getting-by-in-the-gig-economy.

A TaskRabbit's performance statistics only factor in the jobs completed in the previous 30 days, meaning that a tasker who has completed 100 tasks in the last year but who decided to take only one task in December will be immediately outranked by a new tasker who took six that month.

The likelihood is that our app addiction will only progress further. As I mentioned earlier, gig economy applications are still in their infancy. MGI's survey indicates that 30% of working-age Americans are not aware that they can use digital platforms to earn money.[25] Thus, with the proliferation of new app and Web platform options will come an onslaught of new ways to game you into the system.

These markets are utilizing gamification to create a loyal hive of worker bees, preferably ones so fixated on arbitrary rewards and in-app badges that they're never tempted to stray. In case you haven't yet come across the concept, according to Merriam-Webster,

gam·i·fi·ca·tion

noun

the process of adding games or gamelike elements to something so as to encourage participation.[26]

The idea is simple enough: when game elements are applied to a system, people will engage. Tossing a ball back and forth is boring. Earning money for every ball your opponent misses? Now, that might just keep your attention.

---

[25] McKinsey Global Institute. (2016, October). "Independent Work: Choice, Necessity, and the Gig Economy." Retrieved from http://www.mckinsey.com/global-themes/employment-and-growth/independent-work-choice-necessity-and-the-gig-economy
[26] Merriam-Webster Online Dictionary. (2010). "Gamification." Retrieved from http://www.merriam-webster.com/dictionary/gamification.

The success of social media has proven that even when the reward is as abstract as "100 retweets means I'm popular," it's still enough to keep you checking your Twitter account.

Gamification techniques are so universally tempting that a relatively unknown company, Opower, was able to get users to hit up their friends' Facebook feeds about a gamified app that tracked their household electricity output[27]—not something you would usually be raving to the world about.

Likewise, the most successful workplace apps know the power of turning your own statistics into frenzied competition for their benefit, and they do it with colorful interfaces, deceptively simple charts (like Airbnb's Superhost status graphs), and constant reminders of how you compare to the "elite" members of the service.

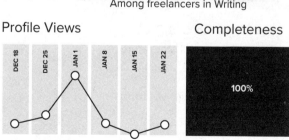

"JOB SUCCESS" STATISTICS. AN APPEALING CHART

Marketing Effectiveness

You've applied to 3 jobs in the past 90 days.
Compared to your peers:

You were:	LESS OFTEN	AVERAGE	MORE OFTEN
Viewed			
Interviewed			
Hired			

Among freelancers in Writing

Profile Views

DEC 18 | DEC 25 | JAN 1 | JAN 8 | JAN 15 | JAN 22

Completeness

100%

[27] Palmer, D. (2012, July 1). "The Engagement Economy: How Gamification Is Reshaping Businesses." Deloitte University Press. Retrieved from http://dupress.com/articles/the-engagement-economy-how-gamification-is-reshaping-businesses/.

Past 30 days

GET TASKING!

If you remain inactive for 90 days, your Tasker status may be suspended.

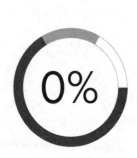

0%

You've accepted **0** of **1** invitations.
Uh oh - your acceptance rate is
significantly below the **75%** standard.

Commitment Rate
No cancellations this year. You're committed!
GOAL: 100% commitment

100%

Response Rate
90 of 90 inquiries requests responded to within 24 hours.
GOAL: At least 90% response rate

100%

Average Overall Rating
GOAL: 4.8 overall star rating

5 Star Trips: 90% of your trips

It's all well and good to strive to be the best on a platform, but you can't let the superficial rewards distract from your primary goals.

Just because you feel rewarded for completing three tasks more than the average tasker doesn't mean that you were paid as much as you should have been for doing them.

Master psychologist B.F. Skinner's birds found that hopping back and forth in front of a scientist was an exciting way to get treats. Then, Skinner changed the variables, and they had to keep hopping, even though the food was being handed out less frequently. Of course, they kept on hopping, searching for treats.[28]

How much time have you spent hopping when you could have flown away and found some real food? The gamification phenomenon within the most popular apps may very well be a Skinner box with a new name.

A digital marketplace, when utilized poorly, becomes a tax on your time and talent. In this economy, and especially once you commit to the freelance life, you have to be aware of what's a stepping stone and what's about to sink you into the river. A dead-end job is never ideal—but they can be especially deadly in the contract world.

[28] Skinner, B. (1947, June 5). "'Superstition' in the Pigeon." Classics in the History of Psychology. Retrieved from http://psychclassics.yorku.ca/Skinner/Pigeon/.

Forbes published a helpful article titled "20 Signs You're Stuck in a Dead-End Job."[29] I've pulled out the eight points I think should wave a red flag in any situation, whether you're a freelance designer, contract hospitalist (i.e. freelance MD), or a handyman:

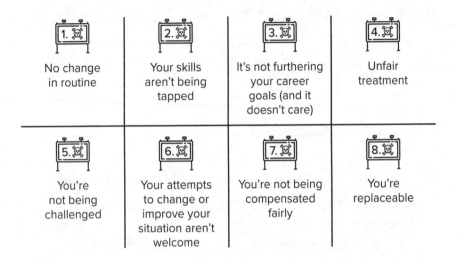

1. No change in routine	2. Your skills aren't being tapped	3. It's not furthering your career goals (and it doesn't care)	4. Unfair treatment
5. You're not being challenged	6. Your attempts to change or improve your situation aren't welcome	7. You're not being compensated fairly	8. You're replaceable

The important thing is this: make sure that most of the project-based jobs you take on help move you forward in some way. You should be making new contacts, challenging your skills, or at least earning enough money from the task to support the former pursuits. Otherwise, you'll just end up treading water.

The Solution

Don't get me wrong. Digital labor markets are still a great resource, especially for those who have little or no experience finding clients outside the app. The key is making sure you're utilizing them as a tool, not a lifeline.

Instead of giving in to temptation and sinking everything you have into one service, you should treat digital marketplaces as one

[29] Smith, J. (2013, November 12). "20 Signs You're Stuck In A Dead-End Job—And What To Do If You Are." *Forbes*. Retrieved from http://www.forbes.com/sites/jacquelynsmith/2013/11/12/20-signs-youre-stuck-in-a-dead-end-job-and-what-to-do-if-you-are/#2715e4857a0b544c6b4a423e

(responsibly) treats dating sites: spread out your online presence, and make sure you're looking out the window, too. You may meet your next flame on the app. Or at the park. Or on another site. Or through your brother. As long as you don't invest too much in any one of those possibilities, you'll be there when it happens.

To help you out, here are five tips you can use to make sure you won't get trapped in the digital marketplace.

TIP 1
Keep your resume, business cards, website, and portfolio up-to-date.

Just because you're not looking for a jobby job doesn't mean you can let your PR slack. Make sure to keep your resume on the cutting edge, put your most recent work in your portfolio, order business cards that reflect what you currently do, and add everything new you do to your professional website. Make sure that your online presence contains a thorough overview about what you do and why you're the best at it; your current resume; a list of services and pricing; testimonials and reviews; a past client roster with logos (if appropriate); an introductory video; and a contact page that lets potential customers reach you a number of different ways. When you actually show up on someone's radar, you'd better make sure they're seeing you at your best.

TIP 2
Memorize your elevator pitch.

The elevator pitch is what you say to Richard Branson (or whatever billionaire is most interesting to you) when he shakes your hand and casually mentions he's looking for a superstar. What exactly do you do, and why are you the best at it? Learn how to say it in under two minutes. If it's good, a potential contact will ask you to elaborate. If they're not interested, then hopefully, your pitch will be memorable enough to pass your name along to the next billionaire.

TIP 3
Practice juggling clients by juggling apps.
If you're good at repairs, why not keep active profiles on Handy and TaskRabbit? Not only will you be meeting a diverse clientele from different platforms, you'll also be able to pick up insight about how much people will pay for particular jobs when you strike out on your own.

TIP 4
Be open to new opportunities.
It'll probably be a long time before you're stable enough to start saying "no" to offers. Network often and, when a job gets offered, be prepared to accommodate. Realistically, you won't be able to take on every assignment, but you will learn 100% more by squeezing room in your Saturday for a once-in-a-lifetime assignment than you will by not doing it.

TIP 5
Form relationships.
You never know at the beginning of a job whether it will be a quick payday or the first day of a years-long partnership. As an employer, I'm quick to decide whether or not someone is a good fit based on how they choose to handle a basic assignment. If I hire a contractor who gives me just the minimum, then I'm not going to waste time giving them a follow-up assignment. If someone gives me gold, however, you can bet I'm going to keep their number. As always, it comes down to knowing your strengths and delivering consistent high-quality work.

The Data

IIIIIIIIIIIIIIIIIIIIIIIIIIIIIIIIIIIIIIIIIIIIIIIIIIIIIIIIIIIIIIIIIIIIIIIIIIIII

In the simplest terms, not being a slave to the app means using relevant sites to maximize career opportunities while minimizing dependence on any one system.

McKinsey Global Institute's analysis came to a similar conclusion.[30] They believe that online talent platforms have the potential to shorten the duration of unemployment for as many as 230 million people by 2025. Likewise, companies willing to use online talent platforms to identify and recruit candidates could reduce human resource costs by 7%. However, they argue that the real strength of these platforms is in the volume of information they gather regarding both individual workers and projects, and their capacity to synthesize this data to match individuals to job opportunities.

If you're interested in discovering how well you fit in with certain "workplace archetypes," check out Good.co and download the app. With just a few short quizzes, you'll be able to judge your compatibility with a long list of employers, who themselves are divided into specific "company personalities." It's more entertaining than enlightening, really. As with most personality tests, the results should be taken with a grain of salt—but it can give you something interesting to ponder.

Discover Yourself

Previous Question:

On a long train, you find yourself sitting next to a stranger. You:

Put on headphones   Chat it up

1 of 18 Questions

Does it drive you nuts when people don't set the time on the microwave?

Why would it?   Totally annoying!

PERSONALITY QUIZ (2015).

[30] Manyika, J. (2015, June). "A Labor Market that Works: Connecting Talent with Opportunity in the Digital Age." McKinsey & Company. Retrieved from http://www.mckinsey.com/insights/employment_and_growth/connecting_talent_with_opportunity_in_the_digital_age

Considering the current focus on compatible company culture when seeking full-time employment, I imagine that we're going to be seeing more employee-employer matchmaking apps like this in the future.

To sum it all up, traditional routes of finding work still exist but are being rapidly undermined by the rise of the digital marketplace. The odds of meeting your next client (or boss) through a short-term job on Fiverr is now just as good as meeting them at Starbucks.

Taking It to the Next Level

So let's say you do everything right: you've outlined your UVP, used it to ace jobs on multiple platforms, kept your resume updated along the way, and now truly hit it off with one of your clients. What's next for that relationship?

☑ 1. Wait until the time is right.
Whether you've been working with a small business or a larger corporation, it's difficult to know when it's time to ask about "joining the family." Some level of intuition is key, as well as common sense. Obviously, it's better to ask after you have just nailed a project, rather than after a few months without contact. Of course, if you have regular correspondence and things are going well, try mentioning that you're able and willing to take on more work. In general, companies prefer giving assignments to people they already know before scouring the job market, which gives you a leg up.

☑ 2. Tell them what else you can do well.
Once you've done a job for someone, there's a tendency to become pigeonholed. If you paint a bathroom as a task, you're going to be thought of as a painter, even though you may also

know how to do plumbing and basic electrical work. Most bosses won't think to ask what other skills you have. So it's up to you to share your talents. When you mention your future availability, offer suggestions for other ways you can assist. Get creative with your ask.

☑ 3. Find out whether the position you hope for even exists.

Before you start the conversation with your client, outline for yourself what you imagine the ideal employment situation to be. Consider this a guideline, however; the more flexible you are with a potential job description, the more likely you'll be able to get your foot in the door. Say you're really hoping for a full-time job, but the company can only afford to hire you part time at the end of the quarter. Once you're employed, though, they might find themselves giving you more tasks than can be fit into a part-time schedule. They may decide the value of your work offsets the cost of paying you for more hours, allowing you to move into the position you wanted all along.

☑ 4. Show your value and make sure you deliver.

If you are given a chance, be sure to give it your all. The goal is always to be more than good—you have to be exceptional. Underpromise and overdeliver, because every single task still reflects on your personal brand.

☑ 5. Maintain a freelancer mindset.

Consider that the average worker now stays at a job for 4.4 years.[31] With statistics like that, it's wise to keep thinking with a gig mentality. After all, once you're back out on the market, you might be back to square one in freelance-land.

☑ 6. Practice the polite decline.

It's always possible that someone might offer you a position that

[31] Kamenetz, A. (2012, January 12). "Generation Flux: The Four-Year Career." *Fast Company*. Retrieved from http://www.fastcompany.com/1802731/four-year-career

you don't have time for or one you know would ultimately be a poor fit. When that happens, be upfront: thank them for the opportunity, but let them know that you're not interested at this time. Never leave them guessing—it's unprofessional and could easily damage your reputation.

EXPERIENCES OF A TOKEN FREELANCER

I've had an interesting time in the wild world of the freelance economy. After leaving a traditional job, I held all of the following positions, most simultaneously, over a six-month period:

- *Summer teacher*
- *Nanny*
- *Hotel maid*
- *Romance writer*
- *Upwork editor*
- *TaskRabbit tasker*
- *Personal assistant*

These gigs involved doing all of the following things (with my college degree in tow):

- *Dog sitting*
- *Scrubbing toilets*
- *Being a bouncer*
- *Installing appliances*
- *Stacking crates*
- *Bungee jumping*
- *Telemarketing*
- *Setting up email marketing campaigns*
- *Chauffeuring*
- *Tutoring*
- *Organizing*
- *And a lot of other little things*

But of all the hoops I've had to jump through, the most frustrating was the scant 30-minute window given for responding to TaskRabbit tasks. Once, I was in the middle of hanging 25 picture frames in an undecorated office building, and despite having my phone in my back pocket, after two hours of pounding nails into drywall, I discovered I was 10 minutes late to respond to two new TaskRabbit assignments. They had been reassigned to other people. And that's just the way it goes.

~ Emma, The Eccentric Assistant

Spotlight: Jennifer the Nanny

During my research, I was pleasantly surprised to meet Jennifer, a 20-something nanny, who found long-term employment through Care.com. She has the charming and approachable personality you'd expect from someone who spends eight hours a day with a two-year-old. Despite not having a formal degree, she now makes a decent living doing what she loves: taking care of children. "Being a nanny was something I'd aspired to for a long time." Jennifer told me. "When I started, I'd been working with children for about eight years . . . so I think that definitely helped me get the job."

Although she wasn't short on experience, Jennifer was struggling to find her first full-time job with a family.

She signed up for both SitterCity and Care.com at once. She explained that it was about four months before she started finding clients through Care, and longer before anyone contacted her on SitterCity. Fortunately, she was able to support herself during the wait by taking a job at a local child care center.

Even so, Jennifer didn't stop hoping she would find a "forever family." Once employed, she was able to afford the subscription required to become a featured Care.com caretaker; only then did she start getting offers. Of course, it would take some trial and error before she found the right fit.

Some experiences were just dismal. "There was one family that I tried to work for where the father made me feel like the help . . . He just wasn't very kind or friendly. So, we discussed if we would like to pursue this and continue on, and I didn't want to. It wasn't working out, and I was extremely happy that they wanted to go on with someone else."

She knew not to settle for the first thing to come along. And, thankfully, it wasn't long before she received an offer from her current employer: a work-from-home mom in need of someone to entertain her child while she juggled clients. After meeting her, Jennifer was confident enough to leave her job at the child care center and take on the role. Now, she says the long process was worth it.

"Any time you're looking for a job that has as much of an impact—honestly, waiting isn't the worst. You'll eventually find someone to work for who you don't mind spending a majority of your time with."

For Jennifer, the digital platform was only ever a supplement to her job-finding process. Even now, she's critical of some aspects of Care.com, particularly the fact that you have to pay to be recognized. (After all, it can be counterintuitive to ask people in need of work to pay to find work.) When the time comes to move on once again, Jennifer has the advantage of knowing how to use the tools of the digital marketplace to land on her feet.

⇨ DO **THIS** / NOT **THAT** ⇦

***Do:*:** Start to optimize your social media presence, preparing yourself for any informal (or formal) networking opportunities.

While you're putting together a fantastic profile on Freelancer.com, take the time to update your LinkedIn, cleanse your Facebook of any questionable pictures, and decide how much you want to risk a potential employer finding you on Twitter.

Don't: Set it to private and think that you're safe.

I cannot state clearly enough: there is no such thing as a private setting on a social website or app. There's simply no way of knowing what a potential client will be able to see or discover about you personally. Thinking broadly about your online brand is the first step toward taking control of your professional life.

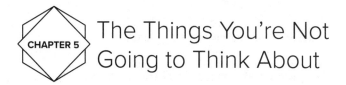

The Things You're Not Going to Think About

For those of you who came from a desk job, where things like vacation and lunch were part of the system, the lack of benefits in the freelance economy is going to feel like a slap in the face. You won't have the same labor law protections offered traditional employees, and you'll probably underestimate your taxes at first. You want healthcare? A retirement account? Time off when your kids come down with a cold? Those things are going to be 100% your responsibility.

Of course, even in career positions, the days of the pension, fully covered company healthcare, and paid vacations are going the way of the dodo. Recent trends indicate that responsibility for benefits is shifting to the worker, regardless of their role. "We've seen for well over a decade a shift towards where employees are just having to pay more," said Laura Sejen, a practice leader at Towers Watson, a human resources consulting firm, in a *Los Angeles Times* article.[32] Between 2000 and 2011, healthcare costs for employees grew 188%, while earnings grew just 44%.

Some of the unspoken hurdles of gig life can be difficult—but only because most people aren't forewarned about the realities of leaving the nine-to-five behind. I've identified seven major areas that most freelancers don't properly prepare for when they first set out:
1. Time Management
2. Boundaries
3. Bookkeeping *(from invoicing to budgeting & taxes)*
4. Self-Improvement
5. Investing
6. Isolation
7. Benefits

[32] Semuels, A. (2013, April 7). "The Numbers Behind the Decline in Workplace Benefits." *The Los Angeles Times*. Retrieved from http://articles.latimes.com/2013/apr/07/business/la-fi-mo-numbers-decline-workplace-benefits-20130407.

1. Time Management

Flexible clients might give you an extension on your deadline, but for most freelancers—especially those just starting out—contracts follow a pay-on-delivery schedule. You're free to take as much time off as you want, but that is time you're not getting paid . . . and that adds up fast.

On the other hand, while working until you drop might help you get ahead financially, it won't be long before stress takes its toll—and you'll soon be taking time off whether you want to or not. The best way to tackle time management is the three-pronged approach: schedule your work days, add in breaks, and adhere to the plan.

Schedule Your Work Days

You'll find that a lot of the "freedom" of working for yourself isn't as free as you might think. Sure, you don't have to work 12-hour days, but if that's the only way the deadline is getting met, then those are the hours you're going to work. This is the fate of most procrastinators—and they don't tend to last long. The best way to avoid a grueling time crunch is to draw up what your working hours are going to look like at the beginning of a project, then stick to them as close as possible.

Here are the tools you'll need:

A CALENDAR YOU LOOK AT REGULARLY:
It doesn't matter if it's Google Calendar, iCal, or a cat-meme Page-A-Day. Pick one and keep it close. Fill it with all your appointments, deadlines, errands, and anything else you need to remember. DO NOT resort to mental note taking. You will forget, and a freelancer can't afford to forget.

A TASK LIST:
Calendars should be used only for scheduling. To manage all the things you need to do daily, you can never have too many lists. But, just like your calendar, make sure that your lists are in a place where you look at them often. That means, try not to let them get buried under the rest of your work. I keep a running "weekly at-a-glance family calendar with to-dos sidebar" in the cloud—which tends to get pretty lengthy—and a daily task list on a whiteboard right next to my computer. You are welcome to use my weekly at-a-glance calendar template, available as a google sheet here: ChunkofChange.com/gigisup

AN ALARM CLOCK:
Just because there's no attendance policy doesn't mean you shouldn't hold yourself accountable for waking up on time. Treat it just like any other job: set your alarm to make sure you start promptly. Keep in mind that you should listen to your own body's clock when scheduling your work schedule. Not all people are productive at 7:00 a.m., and some people do need a one-hour midday nap to feel adequately recharged for the evening ahead. Give yourself permission to fall out of sync with the corporate work day; after all, you are your own boss now.

Schedule Your Breaks
For the workaholics among us, it can be tempting to let Friday's work spill over into Saturday and unfinished Saturday work spill into Sunday. It's in your best interest not to let this happen. So long as you're getting everything done that you need to, you should schedule (at least) one day of your week as your own personal weekend, giving yourself time to walk away and relax . . . and, of course, get some chores done so that the little things in your life don't pile up.

It's also to your advantage to schedule your rest days on Saturday and Sunday, aligning with the traditional work world. This will help you stay in sync with friends and clients, who might not be able to make time for you during your scheduled break of Tuesday afternoons. Plus, the more aligned you are with the traditional work world, the more you'll feel naturally obligated to stick to a self-imposed routine.

Depending on your temperament, you might find it beneficial to schedule breaks during the day. Giving yourself a consistent lunch hour can give you incentive to get to XYZ on the early side, and you'll return from your midday meal with a fresh mind to get started on the next chunk of work.

Stay On Task

All of the preparation in the world falls apart if you aren't able to stay focused during the time you've allotted to finish your assignments. While most people can sit down and finish things without clicking over to Facebook every fifteen minutes, I know a lot of creative types that struggle with the limitless freedom of being able to work in their PJs. They open YouTube for what they promise themselves is just one music video, but before they know it, they've watched every other trending clip . . . and now it's time for dinner. So, what can you do?

TIME TRACKING:
Sometimes it's enough just to recreate the stress of your boss looking over your shoulder to channel your guilt into productivity. If you're an Upwork writer, their desktop app has this built in: once you turn on "task tracking," the application will take a screenshot of your desktop every five minutes, documenting exactly what you're doing with those hours you've contracted through your client. For something slightly less invasive, there's also RescueTime, a background app that tracks exactly how much time you spend

active on website tabs, messaging services, and other applications. You can choose to receive daily, weekly, or monthly reports of your activity, which can be useful for invoicing or just seeing how well you're keeping to your own schedule.

DISTRACTION BLOCKERS:
If you're suffering from a particularly debilitating addiction to social media, there are browser extensions that will block you from your favorite sites during the work day. If you decided you're going to work every day from 10:00 a.m. to 6:00 p.m., download an app like LeechBlock (Firefox), StayFocused (Chrome), ColdTurkey (Windows), or Mindful Browsing (Safari) and set them to be active during that time. Sure, you can forcibly deactivate these apps, but it won't be the app's fault that you have no self control.

FOCUS TIMERS (THE POMODORO TECHNIQUE):
Some people like to utilize the Pomodoro Technique to keep themselves on task: 25 minutes of work, 5 minutes of break.[33] This method has become so popular there are apps for it on virtually every platform; almost every focus timer on the market utilizes this technique, but any clock with a buzzer will give you the same effect. It requires some discipline to actually stick to the five minute breaks though.

The Burnout Problem
Why do we need breaks? A weekend? Because the risk of burning out is very real. The American Psychological Association describes job burnout as "an extended period of time where someone experiences exhaustion and a lack of interest in things, resulting in a decline in their job performance."[34] Burnout can sneak up on you.

[33] Cirillo, F. (2011). *The Pomodoro Technique*. Berlin: Cirillo Consulting GmbH.
[34] Gerry, L. (2013, April 1). "10 Signs You're Burning Out—And What to Do About It." *Forbes*. Retrieved from http://www.forbes.com/sites/learnvest/2013/04/01/10-signs-youre-burning-out-and-what-to-do-about-it/#a696ca35e01a.

After one, two, or five weekends of working overtime—and getting results—it's tempting to think that you can keep it up indefinitely. Then, the weeks wear on and you start to forget things, and you start to dread the assignments at hand, and before you know it, you start sleeping through your alarm and missing deadlines. And you aren't sure exactly what went wrong.

Lisa Gerry of *Forbes* wrote an article about her own experience with burnout.[35] For her, it was "multiple, chronic stressors over an extended period of time" that did her in, rather than any one incident. The symptoms she uses to characterize burnout include exhaustion, lack of motivation, cognitive problems, slipping job performance, and health problems—all things that can quickly take a toll on your ability to make ends meet.

Burnout is a sign of prolonged neglect of self. As much as we might try to make time to relax, the truth is, the stresses of the modern world tend to push self-care to the bottom of our radars. If your overall lifestyle is sedentary and you're not eating well, even regular breaks aren't enough to prevent burnout from setting in. Sometimes the biggest change that needs to happen when pursuing a freelance lifestyle is an internal one: What can you do to make sure you're healthy enough for the long haul?

There are a number of solutions, but the easiest one for most people is to take up some form of exercise. This doesn't have to involve the gym. Take the dog for a walk, pull up a yoga video on YouTube, ride your bike to the market, or pump some free weights in your garage. Just get moving.

Also remember to see your doctor(s) regularly and engage in as much preventive care as you can. For some of us, this means seeing a therapist regularly, too. Just find balance wherever you can.

---

[35] Gerry, L. (2013, April 1). "10 Signs You're Burning Out—and What to Do About It." *Forbes*. Retrieved from http://www.forbes.com/sites/learnvest/2013/04/01/10-signs-youre-burning-out-and-what-to-do-about-it/#a696ca35e01a

2. Boundaries

It's one thing to be sitting in a cubicle with your boss checking in at regulated times; it's another when your deadline is "sometime this Friday" and your primary communication method is Facebook Messenger. When the line between professional and casual becomes blurred, unspoken boundaries become the new measure of success for freelancer-client relationships. Although some of these shouldn't need to be said, here are a handful of things that can throw a wrench in a budding freelance relationship.

FAILING TO KEEP CONTACT LIMITED TO WORKING HOURS:
Even though you might work better at 2:00 a.m., chances are your client doesn't. Keep your email and text message updates limited to traditional work hours, because a phone buzzing on the client's nightstand before dawn could kill an otherwise solid relationship. Consider drafting that email at night and waiting to hit the send button until you're back at your desk in the morning.

INAPPROPRIATE TOPICS OF CONVERSATION:
When it comes to personal questions, if you wouldn't ask something of your Great Aunt Sue, you probably shouldn't ask it of your client. While it's likely you'll someday want to get to know them better, it's better to ask too little than too much. The converse is true as well. If asked about your personal life, keep it short and sweet.

CONTACTING A CLIENT THROUGH PRIVATE LINES (THAT THEY DID NOT GIVE YOU ACCESS TO):

Sally's client is running late, but all Sally has to get in touch with the client is his email address. She snoops and finds his cell phone number on Facebook and takes it upon herself to give him a call to see where he is. The client is unnerved by this invasion of privacy and, after the meeting, never contacts Sally again. Don't be like Sally. Respect everyone's privacy (and their desired methods of communication), and keep your correspondence on predetermined channels.

3. Bookkeeping

|||||||||||||||||||||||||||||||||||||||||||||||||||||||||||||||||||||||||||||

No one likes to stay organized all of the time. But being a freelancer means you either get organized or get robbed. Remember: you are your own bookkeeper—until you make enough money to afford to outsource the task, that is. Fortunately, there are a lot of online tools and apps out there to assist you in keeping track of all of the details. My friend, Artin Aghamalian, who owns D-Vision Inc. Bookkeeping Services, shared a list of his favorites for your benefit.

Invoicing

WHAT IT IS: An invoice is a list of goods sent or services provided, with a statement of the sum due for these; a bill.

WHY IT MATTERS: Once you finish a project or task, you'll need to send the client an invoice. Then it's your job to keep track of when you sent it to the client and when they paid it.

PRO TIP: A lot of the freelancers I help have terrific work ethics; they have no problem getting jobs done. Billing for their hours, however, is a different story. My suggestion is to set one day each month (the 15th, say) to handle invoicing. When your clients get a bill at the same time every month, they're more likely to pay in a timely manner. Just be sure to track your hours throughout the month, as you go, using one of the helpful tools listed below.

TOOLS TO USE:
FreshBooks | TSheets | Viewpost

Receipts

WHAT IT IS: A receipt is a written acknowledgment of having taken into one's possession a specified amount of money, goods, etc.

WHY IT MATTERS: For tax purposes, you'll need to keep track of all the money you spend. (Yes, all of it.) This includes lunches with clients, computer upgrades, gas and car repairs, office supplies, and more. You won't be able to claim any of it as a tax deduction unless you keep your receipts (either paper or digital).

PRO TIP: Make a file for all of your receipts and scan them into your computer (or mobile device) monthly. Then upload everything to the cloud to keep it safe and centrally located.

TOOLS TO USE:
NeatDesk | Shoeboxed | Wave | Dropbox
Google Drive

Budgeting

WHAT IT IS: A budget is an estimate, often itemized, of expected income and expense for a given period in the future.

WHY IT MATTERS: Fluctuating income makes it especially important to track what's coming in and what's going out . . . and when.

PRO TIP: Keep track of: (1) money already received, (2) money that should be arriving soon, (3) money going out, and (4) any difference between those numbers. In my opinion, the best way to keep your finances in order is Quickbooks Online, Self-Employed Edition (less than $10 per month). Also, check out the public templates that Google offers for small business budgeting.

TOOLS TO USE:
Quickbooks Online SE | Mint | Google Sheets
Microsoft Excel

Savings and Cashflow

WHAT IT IS: Savings are sums of money for use at a later date.

WHY IT MATTERS: The biggest problem for freelancers is a failure to save for unforeseen expenses (and upcoming taxes!). When your income fluctuates from month to month, you need to be even more prepared than the next gigger for whatever may come your way.

PRO TIP: First of all, be sure to talk to your tax professional and get a projection of next year's tax estimate.

Put money away every month to cover your tax liability. Perhaps more importantly, pay yourself first. Don't make savings your lowest priority; make it your highest priority. You can start small! (Even stashing $50 from each check makes a difference.)

TOOLS TO USE:
Bank of America's Keep the Change Program
America Saves "Tools & Resources"

Retirement

WHAT IT IS: Retirement savings are the income on which a retired person lives.

WHY IT MATTERS: There is no more gold watch at the end of the road—and, as a freelancer, you certainly can't hold your breath waiting for a pension. Unfortunately, you just can't work forever . . . nor should you. So, no matter how old you are, you need to start thinking about retirement planning today.

PRO TIP: You're the ONLY one who's going to keep an eye on your retirement. So go see a professional (preferably, a certified financial planner) to start putting pen to paper . . . and money into the coffers. Start a bona fide retirement account now (e.g. IRA, ROTH, etc.) that you will not touch until retirement age. Remember to watch your social security stats. Oh, and don't forget to diversify!

TOOLS TO USE:
AARP Retirement Calculator
Vanguard Retirement Nest Egg Calculator
RetirePlan App

Taxes

WHAT IT IS: Taxes are the sum of money levied upon incomes and demanded by the government for its support.

WHY IT MATTERS: In order to avoid fines and penalties, you may need to make quarterly estimated tax payments. It sounds scary, but it's better to know in advance than have issues with the IRS later. Even "moonlighters"—those only freelancing on the side—might still need to cough up additional taxes.

PRO TIP: Get an excellent freelance-savvy accountant, and ask him or her questions about how to best prepare for tax season, based on your specific line of work. Ask your CPA for estimated quarterly tax coupons that you pay as you go, throughout the year, lessening your end-of-year burden. My favorite resource for tax questions related to the sharing economy is 1099.is. It's a blog for those on Etsy, eBay, Kickstarter, Airbnb, TaskRabbit, etc.

TOOLS TO USE:
TurboTax
IRS2Go App
1099.is

4. Self-Improvement

||||||||||||||||||||||||||||||||||||||||||||||||||||||||||||||||||||

The one thing people never make enough time for is self-improvement. When you get too entrenched in what you're doing, it can be easy to forget to exercise other parts of your brain. There's also monetary incentive to keep your skills fresh: not only does having a varied portfolio give you an edge when competing for gigs, people with additional skills tend to earn more (even in a traditional work environment). One study found that knowing an extra language is enough to get you a 2% increase in your annual income.[36] In other words, it might be time to brush up on your high school Spanish.

However, unless you're already a pro at time management, committing to a traditional classroom structure to learn something new can be impossible. Fortunately, the digital age has made it easier than ever to take online classes, most of which bend to your schedule. Here are just a handful of websites that can teach you something right now:

⚡ Udemy:
Online courses for virtually every subject, optimized for desktop and mobile learning. Some free, some paid.

⚡ Coursera:
Similar to Udemy with its broad range of subjects and mobile options, but Coursera distinguishes itself by partnering with universities to offer courses taught by real professors. FYI: These courses often come with a price tag.

⚡ MIT OpenCourseWare:
Full course material from MIT, online, for free.

---

[36] Popick, S. (2014, June 4). "Want to Boost Your Salary? Try Learning German." *Time*. Retrieved from http://time.com/money/137042/foreign-language-fluency-pay-salary/

⚡ Khan Academy:
Courses focusing primarily on building-block skills like math, biology, history, etc. that are 100% free.

⚡ Skillshare:
Popular course categories include business, culinary, design, DIY, film, music, photography, technology, and writing (Also a potential revenue source, as mentioned in Chapter 2).

⚡ Lynda.com:
Lynda's catalogue has hundreds of categories and thousands of tutorials. Subscriptions start at $24.99 a month, but Lynda recently began working with public libraries to expand their reach, offering their services for free when accessed through partnered institutions.[37]

⚡ Duolingo:
Learn a new language for free with this gamified app that is both fun and addictive. Even 15 minutes a week can improve your foreign language prowess . . . and build new neural pathways!

If traditional coursework just ain't your thang, you can always subscribe to daily podcasts like National Public Radio, Ted Talks, or History of the World in 100 Objects and fill your YouTube subscriptions with people like MinutePhysics or Veritasium (a channel devoted to science and engineering videos). If nothing else, it'll keep you fun at parties.

---

[37] Lynda.com. 2014, October 17. "Lynda.com Launches LyndaLibrary Offering Unlimited Off-Site Patron Access to Award-Winning Courses Teaching Business, Technical and Creative Skills." Press Release. Retrieved from http://www.lynda.com/press/pressrelease?id=4063

5. Investing

||||||||||||||||||||||||||||||||||||||||||||||||||||||||||||||||||||||||

Wealthy people know how to make their money work for them, and the primary way to do that is with investing. I'm not going to tell you to jump into the deep end; I'm going to tell you to educate yourself. Take an online course, go to a free workshop at a local financial firm, or play a stock simulator like WallStreetSurvivor.com, where you invest fake money in real companies that gain or lose value based on real market data.

Why invest? Aside from the fact that most savings accounts now pay pitiful interest rates, the natural variability of freelance income means that you might not be able to save enough for retirement from your projects alone.

I realize it's hard to stomach the idea of putting money away when you're not sure how the electric bill is getting paid on the 15th. But even $20 a month can add up over time. There are lots of banking tools that allow you to automatically sock money away, which you can then earmark for regular investments.

Done well, investing can give you a nest egg that will grow much faster than a traditional savings account. Just remember: be safe, and never risk all of your money on anything, including the stock market.

6. Isolation

||||||||||||||||||||||||||||||||||||||||||||||||||||||||||||||||||

Although, at first, it might be heaven not having to get dressed for the office or put on a uniform every day, it won't be long before the loneliness sets in.

"Avoiding loneliness while working from home" is so commonly searched on Google that it took me a mere 0.41 seconds to yield 13.5 million results.

Personally, one way I handle loneliness is by virtually seeing people that I meet with regularly and connecting to them via FaceTime, rather than just on the phone or through email and text. I cannot emphasize enough the connection this simple "face time" provides as a truly healthy lifeline in my weekly work life.

FaceTime might just be enough for me to stave off the feeling of being disconnected; for others, the answer may be getting out. Coworking spaces (e.g. WeWork)—usually a shared working environment with desks available to rent—have been surging with the freelance economy.

According to data from the Global Coworking Survey, "more than 110,000 people currently work in one of the nearly 2,500 coworking spaces available worldwide."[38] At this point, the likelihood that

---

[38] Foertsch, C. (2013, April 4). "New Coworking Spaces Per Work Day." Deskmag. Retrieved from http://www.deskmag.com/en/2500-coworking-spaces-4-5-per-day-741

someone can find a coworking space in their price range, in their area, is pretty good. Obviously, it depends on where you live, but on average, you can rent a desk for anywhere from $150 per month to $450 per month.

Working in a shared space has a lot of potential. Though you may have to deal with increased distractions, there are networking opportunities, technological resources (like printers and copiers), and sometimes even social events.

Spaces like WeWork offer communal sitting areas (with couches, floor pillows, and bar stools), open-air patios, free-flowing beer on tap, and fancy coffee stations. These coworking spaces aren't just practical; they're downright cool.

As an added bonus, once you get familiar with the coworking environment, you'll probably meet some lunch buddies to help break up your day. When you're meeting new people sharing a similar lifestyle, it encourages you to rise to the occasion, keeping your freelance work hours as productive as they can be.

7. Benefits

The biggest problem with working for yourself remains the question of benefits. For better or worse, the United States has tied its social safety net to the traditional employer/employee model, a fact that causes plenty of headaches for people who find themselves outside company lines. At least, for now.

Although the Affordable Care Act has expanded the reach of general health care to more of the population, things like dental, optometry, and psychiatric care tend to require separate considerations. Which brings us to . . .

The Data

||||||||||||||||||||||||||||||||||||||||||||||||||||||||||||||||||||||||||||||||

Benefits, in general, have been drying up lately. According to Mary Meeker's 2015 Internet trends, employer-sponsored retirement plans decreased 10% from 1979 to 2012—from 69% sponsorship to only 59% sponsorship. Healthcare is shifting away from employers as well, at just 54% in 2015 compared to 64% sponsorship in 1999.[39] That means that even if you're holding onto your corporate job, chances are one in two that you're not being covered by a traditional benefits package.

Part of this might be due to what author Steven Hill calls the "Uberization of work," wherein temp positions have become less temporary in the aftermath of the Great Recession. According to federal data, temps have provided one-fifth of the total national job growth since 2008,[40] and most temps are exempt from employee benefits. Corporations treat their temps the same way Uber treats

Virginia Senator Mark R. Warner and Representative Suzan DelBene of Washington aim to fix that problem and provide the gig economy with the stability of portable benefits packages . . .
Have benefits, will travel!

[39] Meeker, M. (2015, May 27). *Internet Trends 2015—Code Conference*. Kleiner Perkins Coufield & Byers. Retrieved from http://kpcb.com/InternetTrends
[40] Hill, S. (2015, October 19). "Creating a New Kind of Safety Net for the Uber Economy." *Fast Company*. Retrieved from http://www.fastcoexist.com/3052433/creating-a-new-kind-of-safety-net-for-the-uber-economy

its drivers: like businesses of their own and, therefore, responsible for their own upkeep.[41]

In a press release announcing the Portable Benefits for Independent Workers Pilot Program Act, Sen. Warner commented that whether by choice or necessity, a growing number of Americans are working without a safety net and have difficulty planning and saving for retirement, health care needs, or on-the-job injuries. The nature of work is changing rapidly, but our policies largely remain tied to a 20th century model of traditional full-time employment. The Act gives the Department of Labor $20 million for grants to states, local governments, and nonprofits for pilot projects to design, implement, and evaluate portable benefits that can move from job to job. You know, portable. The idea is that a person can pay into a fund, much like the current system for unemployment and disability, but their benefits will not be tied to their employer. So when it's off to the next gig, your sense of security comes along for the ride.

The program encourages models that will provide traditionally work-related benefits and protections like retirement savings, workers' compensation, life or disability insurance, sick leave, training and educational benefits, healthcare, and more. The introduction of this brand-spanking-new baby bill shows the demand from both the House and Senate to take care of the American worker in a way that is forward thinking. It is too early to tell if this will be viewed as a partisan effort that just "taxes" us all. I hope not. I hope that both sides can come to a consensus on taking care of people when companies no longer offer them benefits.

Until the political revolution comes along and gives self-employed workers their own social safety net, you're going to have to create your own benefits package.

The Freelancers Union website provides helpful means for signing up for health plans, dental, liability, disability, life, and travel

[41] Asher-Schapiro, A. (2015, December 10). "That Little Lawsuit Against Uber Just Got Bigger—And Could Take Down the Sharing Economy." Uber Lawsuit. Retrieved from http://uberlawsuit.com/That%20Little%20Lawsuit%20Against%20Uber%20Just%20Got%20Bigger.pdf

insurance. The Affordable Care Act makes it easier to shop for health insurance based on income and personal health needs. In many states, you can also qualify for financial subsidies.

Consider it your own personal quest to make sure you're covered. Take time to research what a bare minimum package will cost you, shop monthly prices, and factor that into your freelance budget. Make it a goal to bring in at least that much money for income. Whatever you do, don't risk going without. Landing in the hospital without medical coverage is the priciest thing you can do.

Spotlight: Digital Nomads

I was more surprised than anyone when my first book, *Sell Local, Think Global*, was localized for Indonesia. As a proud SoCal native, the business trends of Indonesia were the last thing on my radar (not that I wasn't thrilled, of course). Yet once I discovered that Bali has become a mecca for the digital nomad movement, my disbelief became excitement. As a freelancer myself, the idea of being able to pack up my work and take it with me across the world—vacationing and getting work done—sounded too good to be true.

The *International Business Times* defines digital nomads as "professionals who are independent of specific locations, who use a Web-based toolkit of Skype, Google Docs and social media to work and collaborate from wherever, whenever."[42] And, it turns out, they're setting up across the globe. Popular digital nomad hubs include Chiang Mai, Thailand; Ho Chi Minh City, Vietnam; and Cebu, Philippines; as well as Buenos

---

[42] Johanson, M. (2014, March 25). "For Digital Nomads, Work Is No Longer a Place and Life Is an Adventure." *International Business Times*. Retrieved from http://www.ibtimes.com/digital-nomads-work-no-longer-place-life-one-big-adventure-1563396

Aires, Argentina and Sao Paulo, Brazil.[43] Another blog lists places like Morocco, Iceland, and even the Galapagos Islands as potential docking sites for the digital nomad.[44]

Turns out Bali is particularly popular, with their coworking spaces Hubud (Hub-in-Ubud) and Lineup Hub actively marketing to an English-speaking audience. Their websites are approachable, modern, and well-maintained. Hubud's promotional video has a pitch that's hard to resist:

"Imagine working in a building made of bamboo, looking out to a rice field, in Bali. Surrounded by people who are techies, entrepreneurial . . . that's paradise."[45]

Curious about just who sets up business in Bali, I uncovered the work of Dr. Dani. While her blog mostly talks about the mind-body health movement, she always speaks glowingly about the freedom to split her time between her wellness center in Bali and home base, Vancouver, Canada. After breaking her hand in a motor accident, she says it was the atmosphere at Bali that helped her heal, "through a combination of daily Balinese massages, daily gentle walks in nature, snuggling with [her] cat, and creating a meditative healing space . . . with meditation tracks, comfy pillows, and minimal technology."[46]

The fact that we live in an age where a medical doctor is no longer confined to an office space is surreal; I still remember when the idea of calling someone in Indonesia for more than 10 minutes was out of the budget.

[43] Johanson, M. (2014, March 25). "For Digital Nomads, Work Is No Longer a Place and Life Is an Adventure." *International Business Times*. Retrieved from http://www.ibtimes.com/digital-nomads-work-no-longer-place-life -one-big-adventure-1563396
[44] Twago. (2015, June 9). "5 Coworking Locations that Will Make You Want to Go Freelance." Retrieved from http://www.twago.com/blog/5-coworking-locations-that-will-make-you-want-to-go-freelance/
[45] Hubud Bali. (2015, June 16). *Hubud: A New Way of Working*. Indonesia: Youtube https://www.youtube.com/watch?v=faBad-JxWh0
[46] Dr. Dani. (2015, August 17). "I Broke My Hand and May Never Do Downward Dog Again- But I Will Survive." Retrieved from http://askdrdani.com/broken-hands-no-more-downward-dog-and-reinvention/

And it turns out, the movement goes across the generational divide. On the digital nomad subreddit, a conversation asking the age range of digital nomads has prompt responses from 40-year-olds, people in their mid-30s, and even a few couples in their 20s who take their children with them wherever they end up.[47]

What's the appeal? A lot of it is the wanderlust—a fancy word that literally means "a strong desire to travel." And even that term has been increasing in popularity in recent years, according to Google.

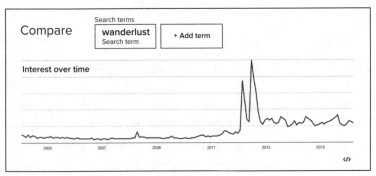

IGNORING A SPIKE IN 2012 WHEN PAUL RUDD MADE A MOVIE ABOUT IT. [48]

I think it goes deeper than just a need to travel. Like any freelancer, no doubt these people came up against the loneliness of working for themselves and took matters into their own hands: instead of a coworking space, they were willing to pack it all up into a suitcase, buy a plane ticket, and decide that if they were going to work for themselves, then they might as well work somewhere beautiful. And they continue to do so, despite drawbacks like having to negotiate with clients across time zones and trouble finding a stable Internet connection. If you ask me, that's the sort of freedom that the American worker has always wanted.

Who knows? I might take that trip to Bali after all.

[47] Reddit. (2015, June 7). R/digitalnomad. "What's the age range of digital nomads." Retrieved from https://www.reddit.com/r/digitalnomad/comments/3cbyij/whats_the_age_range_of_digital_nomads/
[48] Wain, D. (Director). (2012). *Wanderlust*. USA: Universal Studios. https://www.reddit.com/r/digitalnomad/comments/3cbyij/whats_the_age_range_of_digital_nomads/

I was raised in the generation where they told us that the harder you work, the more you'll be rewarded: if you work hard in high school, you'll go to a good college, and if you work hard at that good college, you'll get a good job. So I worked hard.

I graduated nineth in a class of 700, after taking every AP class offered, being president of the Writer's Club and the editor of the class newspaper, performing as first chair second violin and as an active high school thespian, starring in three school plays, and traveling with my drama troupe to Edinburgh to perform. During college, I founded two student organizations, served as a radio DJ one semester at 3:00 a.m., and packed my schedule with so many units that I was able to graduate early as a Campuswide Honors student and with Cum Laude recognition. I also kept busy with my independent projects, including an overly ambitious video game derived from my self-published book. No one could tell me to slow down. I had it in my mind that if I ever stopped working, ever took too long to sleep, eat, or feel, then somehow my life would collapse in on itself.

Then bad luck struck, and my first "big girl" job was in an environment where working hard meant very little. In fact, after spending sleepless nights compiling years upon years of company data into a document that my coworkers could read and discuss, my boss took one look at that document, laughed, and told me I was trying too hard. I was kept at the bottom of the totem pole for the entire time I was there, because I was told I "intimidated people." I was given laughable assignments meant to keep me busy. Finally, I quit—but even when I left, the shadow of that time kept following me. My finances dwindled without that stable income as I tried to adjust to the freelance life, all along my inner child screaming, "What have I been working so hard for? Isn't it supposed to get easier?"

The burnout crept in slowly. I let one deadline slip and then another. "What's the point?" the inner voice started to say. "Working hard never got you anywhere." This continued, until it got to the point that I was weeks late on an assignment, and I no longer had enough money to feed myself. The pay-on-delivery aspect of the freelance life catches up to you fast. Even then, the thought of sitting down at my computer and working made me burst into tears. My resume was so out of date and my soft skills so underdeveloped I knew I was beyond getting a real job. I wanted a vacation I could no longer afford. I knew I wanted someone to save me, but this was the real world, and there's no one to whisk you away when you've spent a lifetime burning up your inner resources. That's what burnout is, I learned: it's when your body finally says "enough," and there's nothing you can do about it.

All I can say is that it took time. Weeks upon weeks, pooling together resources as if by miracles, until my body finally reset and I was able to face the world again.

Oddly enough, what helped was the flight to Ireland I had booked for myself a year before, when I still had that stable job.

I had no plan except to put myself on a farm for a month and do my best to breathe after being worn out by the rat race. It let me see that even though life looked nothing like I had been promised, it could be more than that.

I'm still recovering from the burnout; bouncing back from a prolonged period of ignoring your basic needs doesn't happen overnight. But it's definitely getting better, and working to become a true digital nomad is what's keeping me going.

~ Emma, The Eccentric Assistant

⟦⇨ DO **THIS** / NOT **THAT** ⇦⟧

Do: Try to figure out ahead of time what kind of benefits you're going to have to handle on your own.

Maybe you've always had perfect teeth and have no need for a dental plan, but you're always getting colds and know you need some kind of health coverage. Maybe you're single and don't have any need for life insurance, or perhaps you're a homeowner with a family to provide for. Whatever your scenario, sitting down to draw up your "needs" and "don't needs" before you start shopping will save you time in the long run.

Don't: Be afraid to seek outside help.

You don't have to do everything on your own. There are insurance brokers and retirement planners out there just waiting to help you out. Even if it's just calling your mom for some loving encouragement or going to H&R Block for some beginners tax advice, outside support can go a long way to keeping you from getting overwhelmed. When in doubt, toss up a Facebook or LinkedIn status update asking for the kinds of referrals you need. We're in an interconnected world. Use it to your advantage!

CHAPTER 6
Adding Value & Reaching the Next Level of Your Career

It is possible to make a long-term career out of freelancing—it just doesn't look like the careers of our parents. Now that we've covered what it means to craft your Unique Value Proposition (remember good ol' Chapter 3?), this chapter is about how to take that UVP and put yourself on the path to be exactly as successful as you want to be.

According to a Contently's recent survey of independent writers, consultants, content creators, photographers, designers, videographers, illustrators, and people who did some combination of categories, the freelancers showed a median reported income of $10,001–$20,000 (stay with me; I know what you are thinking, and this will not be you!), including

☑ 19% of respondents who made more than $50,000 in 2014;

☑ 5% who earned six figures.[49]

You could take that to mean that freelancers on average don't make much—however, despite 63.5% of respondents claiming to freelance "full time," 47.1% only completed one freelance project per week, and roughly two-thirds of respondents worked less than 30 hours a week. It begs the question What is full time, really?

Regardless of the number of hours, there's a direct correlation between hard work and increased success. If you want to rise into the camp that earns six figures, you have to make sure you're in the camp that's keeping busy. And to keep busy, you need to keep bringing in new work.

Here are the means to succeed.

[49] Baker, D. (2016, July 5), "Content Study: The State of Freelancing in 2016." Contently. Retrieved from http://contently.net/2016/06/15/trends/how-the-asja-plans-to-stop-being-a-dinosaur/

Always Be Attracting New Clients

||||||||||||||||||||||||||||||||||||||||||||||||||||||||||||||||||||||

We've mentioned before that you have to look beyond the app, but in most cases, you're even going to have to be creative to find your business match. Starting out means doing grunt work: not only do you have to expand past a single platform to reach potential targets, but you should be cultivating a presence across several freelancing platforms that cater to your skill set, and you should be gathering reviews on those platforms as quickly as possible.

Don't shy away from promoting yourself, because boldness means more people are going to notice you, and you never know how long it will take to get the ball rolling. To get you started, consider the following your minimum online presence:

GET ONE	WHY
1. A "Work" Gmail or Cloud-Based Email Address	You must have an easy-to-say-and-spell email account that you can quickly check from your smartphone.
2. LinkedIn	Forget Facebook and Snapchat for a minute and focus on your business contacts instead of your high school clique.
3. Website	Even a one-pager is better than nothing.
4. Online Work Portfolio	Avoid sending attachments when cold-contacting potential clients. People are much more open to clicking .pdf links than they are to downloading a potential virus.
5. Reviews	None of the other must-haves mean much if you don't show off former clients' reviews and testimonials as the ultimate "why choose you" pitch.

Unfortunately, it may take months (or years) of building up a client base before you can turn down a gig. That means that your online profiles and portfolios should be as approachable as possible. While it's tempting to spatter your profile with showings of your dry wit, Harry Potter obsession, and clog collection to display your authenticity, there is definitely a point where you can be too honest.

Keep the Pipeline Moving

Remember that handy calendar from Chapter 5? Make sure that's always full. The Contently survey proves that the more hours you work during the week, the more money you're likely to bring in.

It's basic math: the more projects you finish quickly, the more likely you're getting paid and the more time you have to start new projects to bring in more revenue. Not only that, completed contracts lead to happy customers—and those happy customers usually leave good reviews on your profiles.

Beware: there may be a tendency to stop once you reach your target. A recent study, reported on in *The New York Times*, showed that, with Uber, many drivers "appeared to have an income goal in mind and stopped when they were near it, causing them to knock off sooner when their hourly wage was high and to work longer when their wage was low."[50] It may fly in the face of economic theory, but the stats don't lie.

[50] Scheiber, N. (2016, September 4). "How Uber Drivers Decide How Long To Work." *The New York Times*. Retrieved from http://www.nytimes.com/2016/09/05/business/economy/how-uber-drivers-decide-how-long-to-work.html?_r=0.

Don't be lured into a false sense of security. When it comes to freelance work, there are ebbs and flows—and you must take advantage of the ebbs. When Uber is offering you surge pricing, stick it out and drive an extra hour or two rather than being tempted to clock out just because you've hit your mark for the day. Your bottom line (down the line) will thank you.

Secure Repeat Work

This is going to be a combination of both relationship-building and doing good work. Not only are happy customers more likely to bring you repeat assignments, they're also more likely to be open to another contract—but you have to let them know you're interested.

Usually a simple "I enjoyed working on this; let me know if you have other needs in the future" when you turn in your assignment is enough to get the conversation started. Certain platforms, like TaskRabbit, give you an incentive to rehire a tasker in the form of an automated message that looks like a discount from the tasker himself.

Ben Q.

"Thanks for hiring me for your task! If you'd like to hire me again in the future, check out my profile where you can see all my skills and rates. You'll also get $10 off your next time working with me if you use this referral code: TSK14Y."

AUTO-RESPONSE UPDATE

Take a page from the app, and make sure you follow up with your completed jobs by offering a link to your skills and rates profile on your website and a juicy incentive. (I recommend additional time rather than a discount.)

Most freelancers agree that repeat clients are your bread and butter, so the more you have, the better you'll be doing overall. In short, be friendly, do good work, turn in on time, rinse, and repeat.

Earn Up

||||||||||||||||||||||||||||||||||||||||||||||||||||||||||||||||||||||

Many white-collar workers are self-employed: these are the consultants, the project managers, and other titles that mean more revenue but aren't nearly as unobtainable as you would think. The difference between them and the average Upworker is in how well they know and market their professional skills. It really comes down to your mindset.

An article by *US News* profiled a young consultant, Amanda Boelyn, whose story really shows the potential of aiming upward.[51] In less than three years, Boelyn was able to go from fresh graduate with a certificate in management to corporate consultant, starring as a Target Corporation employee, then working as a Wells Fargo recruiter, and finally accepting her first independent gig at AT&T. She independently maintains half a dozen clients and even found the time to launch her podcast, *She Did It Her Way*, profiling other female entrepreneurs. Although she's surely the exception to the rule, no doubt it was her decision to accept nothing less than she had earned before that allowed her to climb the ladder at so fast a rate. In fact, it was the $10,000 pay cut she took when she left Target to go to Wells Fargo that inspired her to strike out on her own.

However, as much as you should strive to raise the bar for yourself, there's still a right way and a wrong way to give yourself a raise. For instance, there's a big difference between asking existing clients for a raise and learning to ask for more at the beginning of a relationship. You never want to change the price of something in the middle of a project, unless circumstances have changed dramatically. Even if your client agrees to the budget, that's going

[51] Soergel, A. (2015, October 9). "Despite Blurred Lines, Fortune Favoring the Freelance Economy." U.S. News. Retrieved from http://www.usnews.com/news/articles/2015/10/09/fortune-favoring-the-freelance-economy.

to leave a bad taste in their mouth, and you can bet they're going to question whether they want to work with you again.

You also want to keep your own level of experience in mind. Obviously, the more work you have under your belt, the more you can ask for. Once you have enough experience to start asking for a higher pay bracket, make sure you're still being realistic. Regularly scope out competitors who offer the same skills at a similar level of experience, and see for yourself what they charge. You don't want to be much higher or much lower than their numbers. That in mind, bringing in new work is your opportunity to adjust your rates upwards, and eventually you'll be exactly where you imagined you'd be.

Know Your Worth

(i.e. Don't Do Anything for Free)

Not all free work is created equal. I believe that when you're first starting out, volunteering with nonprofits may be the fastest way to build a good professional reputation and a skill set that will help you later on. Sometimes, doing small-scale spec work can help you build your portfolio—as long as it's not going to take you a huge chunk of time to finish it. For the most part though, doing sample work for for-profit organizations is exploitation of your labor. If getting hired is contingent on how fast you finish an entire email campaign for them to look at or on doing a company's market research for them, you should take your skills elsewhere. Someone will pay you to do those things and should respect you enough to do so.

It's important to understand that "why choose you" goes both ways, whether you're a freelancer or an employer. Just as clients are evaluating you for a potential fit, you need to be evaluating your potential employer. Do you want to work long term with someone who expects your labor should be free?

Rather than doing free work, consider offering a discounted rate for first-time clients or a percentage off for prepayment of a block of hours. This offers the same benefits that you might hope to get from spec work, but ensures you're still compensated for the time you put in.

There are times when you might consider offering free work for a company if it means significant exposure; however, there should always be a limit to what you're willing to do.

Target Bigger Clients

In general, if you're doing a good job, the big clients will come to you. It's about planting seeds and having patience. People don't tend to stay in the same position long—as long as you're rubbing elbows at the virtual water cooler, someone you forgot you knew will suddenly get a job at a major studio, then remember that they knew this great freelancer back in the day (you), who would be a perfect fit for the company's new such-and-such.

Of course, if you feel like you're ready to reach for your dream job with Apple, the best thing you can do is make sure you're prepared. Big companies have no patience for little mistakes. Even if your portfolio gets their attention, if you're too disorganized to make the interview or if you're still in the habit of letting things fall through the cracks, that opportunity may be lost for good.

I wouldn't call ohso! design a major company, but I've had my share of unprofessional cold calls. I used to get emails from college students at least once or twice a month asking me whether I had any openings, without doing any research into me or my business. A couple of them even started their emails with "Dear Sir." (Sigh.)

Once you're prepared, however, securing a major client is one of the fastest ways to climb from the middle of the income pool to the coveted six-figure margin. Just make sure you're not jumping into the deep end too soon.

Always Look for New Opportunities

Even if you manage to quickly put together a roster of well-paying repeat clients, make sure you don't get too comfortable. You want to always be expanding your network, or else you'll stagnate professionally. Even in Contently's study, the 10% of freelancers who reported never pursuing new clients earned less than $20,000 a year,[52] which means that there's also a financial risk to settling in. Not to worry—if you're keeping your profiles up to date, garnering reviews from happy customers, and updating your portfolio, it won't be long before new clients are finding you.

No matter what category of freelancing you end up in, you can't go wrong by exceeding expectations. When you do enough good work for enough good people, things have a way of working out in your favor.

[52] Teicher, J. (2015, June 22). Contently Study: "The State of Freelancing in 2015." The Freelancer. Retrieved from http://contently.net/2015/06/22/resources/contently-study-state-freelancing-2015/

The Data

In mid-2015, MBO Partners released a five-year study of freelancing in America, featuring some good news: From 2011 to 2015, the number of independents earning $100,000 or more grew about 45%—a compound annual growth rate of about 7.7%. High earners reported mean revenues of an astonishing $192,000, up 4% from 2014.[53]

What's the recipe for a high-earning freelancer? According to MBO, those who earn more tend to have more experience:

☑ Only 1 out of 10 full-time freelancers working as independents for less than 2 years makes more than $100,000.

☑ Among those with 25 years of experience, 1 in 4 ranks in the over $100,000 category.

However, the study also points out that the general "shift to contingent workers by companies" is creating more work for freelancers who serve these businesses—meaning there's now more of that high-wage pie for everyone.

The Takeaway
Now is your opportunity to reach for the stars . . . and don't be discouraged if you have to put in some years to get there.

[53] MBO Partners. (2015). "MBO Partners State of Independence in America 2015." Retrieved from https://www.mbopartners.com/uploads/files/state-of-independence-reports/MBO-SOI-REPORT-FINAL-9-28-2015.pdf

Spotlight: Sarah the Writer

I've known Sarah for a long time. She's my editor, writing specialist, coffee confidant, and absolutely one of the greatest consultants I know. So of course I called her up to get her perspective on the whole affair: what brought her to the freelance economy, and how did she get so dang good at it?

> "You have to understand, I've done a lot of things," Sarah points out. "I've worked in corporate and at agencies. I was even considering a PhD at one point in order to pursue research."

Not that she has any need for a PhD. Sarah already boasts a certificate in professional publishing from Stanford University and a master's degree in professional writing from the University of Southern California. After leaving corporate America, Sarah quickly rose through the ranks of independent work, even becoming president of the Los Angeles chapter of the Editorial Freelancers Association (EFA) and starting her own agency, Play on Words, whose collective writing team served as many as thirty clients a week. Nowadays, she's stepped back from the agency to write on her own.

She describes herself now as a content strategist, managing the demands of an average of five clients a week with new ones calling in regularly. She's even to the point where she can request prepaid blocks from potential clients by giving them a 5% discount off her standard rate. "You charge what people will pay for your experience. I'm at the point where I don't work for anyone unless it's going to be ten hours," she says. "It's not worth the initial investment of time and comprehension."

Sarah says it was a number of things that brought her to where she is. Like many early adopters of the lifestyle, Sarah held a number of corporate jobs before she figured out traditional employment just wasn't for her.

> "I was always a round peg in a square hole. When I got a full-time job, I was always just the squeaky wheel. The problem is: if you're the employee always pointing out the problem, eventually they assume that you're the problem. But as a consultant, companies appreciate that feedback. I discovered I was always more appreciated as an outsider."

That's not to say that freelancing is always a walk in the park. Even for her, the hardest part is budgeting, and not just money: she describes it as a constant struggle to "budget your time, resources, money, other people you reach out to—just figuring out how to make everything stretch. Because in the freelance world, it's feast or famine. One week it's five jobs, another it's one. And I'm the kind of person that doesn't like to turn work away. I had to learn how to delegate. That's how I ended up starting my agency: I managed to get together a great pool of other freelancers so that if someone came to me and I couldn't do a job, I could give it to someone else and charge a referral fee. I learned how to make the most of every opportunity."

Her story just confirms what I've always said about the power of relationships. Everyone you meet in this realm has the potential to be another link in the chain, whether they end up a client, an employee, a collaborator, or even someone to talk you down after a particularly difficult job. (Sarah's been most of those for me.) There's value in all of it.

You would think that with her successes, Sarah would be above doubts about the independent lifestyle. However, even she sometimes struggles with outside approval.

> "People will always say it's not a real living . . . even though I tell them I work 40 hours a week, and I get paid. And even when I cave in and go work for someone else, I just find out again that I'm that round peg in a square hole. This is what works for me. I always end up coming back to freelancing."

⟦⇨ DO **THIS** / NOT **THAT** ⇦⟧

Do:: Network wherever and whenever you can to keep the fresh leads flowing.

Whether online or offline, it's important to stay active in social spheres and take advantage of networking opportunities. Even if your coffers are full at the moment, you want to set yourself up for future success. Take advantage of any way to rub elbows with new potential clients, whether in the real world or the digital one.

Don't: Try to leech business from a digital marketplace you're a part of. This is ethically (and sometimes legally) problematic.

We haven't talked much about balancing your presence on online workplaces and doing your own work, but there is often overlap—especially when you're getting started—between clients you meet on Upwork / Freelancer / Guru, etc. and the clients you find on your own. This is fine, until you start actively competing with the digital marketplace for similar services. For example: it's okay if, during your time working with TaskRabbit, you find a few handyman clients who want to continue working with you outside the app. It's not OK if you start an agency called Mark's Home Services, use your profile on TaskRabbit to scope out potential clients, then use your profile to redirect queries from their website to yours. Situations like this are rare, but it's a no-no to keep in mind.

CHAPTER 7

FROM FREELANCER TO EMPLOYER:

The Tipping Point

Ideally, even in this economy, a successful freelancer should be able to climb the ladder high enough that they can eventually afford to hire help—even if that "help" is just a maid and a dog walker! It just makes sense that, once you start juggling lots of work, it's a smarter move to pay someone else to do the little stuff. Then you hire someone else, then another person. And, before you know it, you're no longer a freelancer; you're running a business.

For some this is the ideal, but it is not inevitable. First, you should question whether becoming a business is even your end goal. For many, that kind of headache may not be on the docket. If it is, though, you should take steps to make sure you're ready to transition from being your own boss to being *the* boss.

While you don't *need* to employ others to further your career, for many, it is the next logical step.

The Freelancers Union's 2014 survey found that 5% of the freelancers surveyed identified as "Freelance Business Owners." In a few years, you could be one of them.[54]

To that end, this chapter is designed to familiarize you with the realities that small business owners face and uncover the personality traits that help them cope.

---

[54] Horowitz, S. (2014, September 4). "53 Million Americans Are Freelancing, New Survey Finds." Retrieved from https://www.freelancersunion.org/blog/dispatches/2014/09/04/53million/

The Difference:
Independent Freelancer vs. Freelance Business Owner

IIIIIIIIIIIIIIIIIIIIIIIIIIIIIIIIIIIIIIIIIIIIIIIIIIIIIIIIIIIIIIIII

At what point do you involve a secondary worker in your brand? Well, it depends on what types of services you offer. Creative types—artists, writers, designers—often find it just as lucrative to focus on their own craft as it would be to manage other creatives. Running a business usually means less time doing and more time overseeing, so for the freelancer whose joy comes from creative expression, this can be a problem. For someone whose goods are more tangible, however, it can bring exciting possibilities. Rather than solo knitting handmade sock puppets in your garage to fill Etsy orders, you might hire three other knitters to produce while you handle the books and the marketing. Those who offer services (like repairs or errand running) could bring on others to tackle the tasks that don't fit their schedule, charging a fee for the referral.

It doesn't even need to be about creating inventory or expanding services. MBO Partners' survey argues that freelancers' hiring of other freelancers can be indicative of a trend toward greater creative collaboration brought about by the on-demand environment. "In essence, Independents team up with other Independents to pool their talents and address more complex challenges in the marketplace. Banding together with other Independents allows them to compete more effectively with larger firms and offer a broader range of services than they could individually."[55]

It's this new collaboration that leads to "project-specific small businesses," with flexible staffing and virtual offices, wherein the size and nature of the teams gathered fluctuates based on the projects they tackle. These teams rely on cloud technologies to manage themselves and their projects, giving them efficiency and cost

---

[55] MBO Partners. (2015). "MBO Partners State of Independence in America 2015." Retrieved from https://www.mbopartners .com/uploads/files/state-of-independence-reports/MBO-SOI-REPORT-FINAL-9-28-2015.pdf

advantages over traditional business models.

It's here that the dividing line between Freelance Business Owner and Independent gets blurry. A person might put themselves in charge of this sort of venture temporarily—in order to bid on larger projects that they would otherwise be incapable of doing on their own—but then return to solo contracts when the deal is done. As always in the freelance world, there's no shortage of mobility.

How Does Your Personality Match Up?

A surprisingly thorough survey conducted in 2010 by *The Guardian Life Small Business Research Institute* concluded that the following six traits were shared by business owners who ran successful businesses[56]:

Collaborative	Self-Fulfilled	Future-Focused
Curious	Tech-Savvy	Action-Oriented

[56] The Guardian Life Small Business Research Institute. (2010, June). "Six Dimensions That Characterize Success-Oriented Small Business Owners." Retrieved from http://balanceatwork.thomasmarsden.com.au/blog/wp-content/uploads/2011/08/success-oriented-small-business.pdf

Before anyone begins this transition, it's important to determine whether or not those words resonate. But rather than outlining what each means, I thought it would be more helpful if I gave you a short quiz to determine how well you're prepared to manage a business.

The Short Leadership Quiz

|||||||||||||||||||||||||||||||||||||||||||||||||||||||||||||||||||

Question	Answer (Circle One)
Do I thrive in an environment where I am working with others?	Yes / No
Am I happy with my work and the direction I am going?	Yes / No
Do I have a comprehensive One-year plan, including financials?	Yes / No
...a five-year plan, including specific plans for growth?	Yes / No
Do I relish things that are new and unfamiliar to me?	Yes / No
Am I an early adopter and avid daily user of technology?	Yes / No
Do I thrive on getting things done and completing tasks?	Yes / No

Now tally up your score. If you answered "yes" to four or more of the questions above, then you're probably ready to move on to the next step. If not, don't despair. Ask yourself why you answered the way you did. Leadership is a specialized task, and not everyone is well suited to it. It's important to know your own limits and avoid biting off more than you can chew.

Expanding Your Businesses

|||||||||||||||||||||||||||||||||||||||||||||||||||||||||||||||||||||||||

When it comes to building your business, the most important thing is to be properly informed before taking any big steps. For some people, that means signing up for a Udemy / Lynda / Skillshare small business course. Of course, there are other options, too.

My favorite starting point is the local Small Business Development Center (SBDC). Nothing can replace the abundance of information, helpful staffers, free in-person classes, and mentorships with successful local business owners that the SBDC offers regularly. The Small Business Association (SBA) offers an online tool for finding the nearest SBDC in your area.[56]

Don't forget about your local library as a resource as well. Not only are their offerings free, the library also offers a quiet place to work while you work through the stacks of books relevant to the business you're starting!

When it comes to setting up your company legally—the sole proprietor, partnership, LLC, S-corp, or C-corp—each option offers pros and cons as it relates to tax status and legal liability (not to mention perceived credibility). I highly recommend spending two or three hours with a business attorney or CPA in order to decide which format aligns best with your goals.

---

[56] Small Business Association. (2016). "Local Assistance - Small Business Development Centers." Retrieved from https://www.sba.gov/tools/local-assistance/sbdc.

My own company, ohso! design, started as a partnership, but over time, my partner and I realized that our visions for the company weren't matching up. Leaving that arrangement was one of the hardest things I've ever had to do. It was like a divorce—legally, financially, and even emotionally. Bottom line: know what you're getting into before you get there.

Once you're ready to go a bit further down the rabbit hole, start reading. I met lawyer-accountant-guru Mark J. Kohler at a convention, and I've found his blog of advice for entrepreneurs to be a solid resource when it comes to the complex things (e.g. "Why an S-Corporation May Be a Good Move in 2016,"[58] or "Issues to Consider When Creating a Partnership,"[59] just to name a few). For some people, though, it may be enough to spend a few hours on LegalZoom looking at documents.

For me, I have a trusty lawyer friend that is worth every penny.

The Data

The freelance economy is growing and so are the aspirations of the freelance class. According to the MBO Partners study, 16% of freelancers reported that they planned to expand their business over the next two to three years.[60] (In fact, that number rose each year of the five-year study, a significant increase from the 11% that began it.)

Although only 5% of those surveyed by the Freelancers Union identified as Freelance Business Owners,[61] MBO's survey states that 36% of interviewed independent workers hired other independent workers on a contract basis over the previous year

[58] Kohler, M. (2015, November 23). "When to Set Up an S-Corporation." Mark J. Kohler (blog). Retrieved from http://markjkohler.com/why-an-s-corporation-may-be-a-good-move-in-2015/
[59] Kohler, M. (2015, August 25). "Issues to Consider When 'Partnering.'" Mark J. Kohler (blog). Retrieved from http://markjkohler.com/issues-partnering/
[60] MBO Partners. (2015). "MBO Partners State of Independence in America 2015." Retrieved from https://www.mbopartners.com/uploads/files/state-of-independence-reports/MBO-SOI-REPORT-FINAL-9-28-2015.pdf
[61] Horowitz, S. (2014, September 4). "53 Million Americans are Freelancing, New Survey Finds." Freelancers Union. Retrieved from https://www.freelancersunion.org/blog/dispatches/2014/09/04/53million/

The Gig is Up

(up from 9.8% in 2014) and spent a total of $101 billion dollars doing so. That's the equivalent of employing 2.4 million full-time workers via traditional hiring.

According to MBO, the data suggests that these trends demonstrate the potential for independent work as a source of jobs. It's a good sign, considering that the independent workforce is growing more than five times faster than the overall workforce: the number of freelancers increased 27% by the end of the 2015 study, whereas the overall US employment growth stagnated at only 5.4%.

The Takeaway

The shift from freelancer to employer isn't for everyone. But if you have the ambition, temperament, and the willingness to get your ducks in a row, it can be the decisive step between being "just you" and being the boss you always wanted to be.

It's a good time to dream big in the freelance world. Draw up a plan and see how much you could save yourself by investing in an assistant. Start small—virtual assistants are now only a click away—and see what the future brings.

Believe it or not, one of my earliest dreams was of being a business owner. My favorite daydream was of opening a shop that sold chocolates and roses. My clientele would be wide-eyed lovers who would tell me their life stories as they browsed my quaint little storefront, later sending me notes about how happy their fiancé was about the bar and bouquet they decided on. (What can I say? I'm a hopeless romantic.)

It wasn't entirely a pipe dream. I did look into what it meant to take out a small business loan, compared some prices for a potential location, and asked local florists how they got their stock. Thing is, I didn't factor in my own temperament to the feasibility of my dream: I'm shy, reclusive, and terrible at haggling. I soon realized that I'm just not cut out for the cutthroat world of retail.

As a freelancer, I find I enjoy taking on assignments and handing them back to an authority figure. There's security in knowing that I'm not the one calling the shots— it's just the way I am.

Moral of the story: get to know yourself first. It's okay if you're not the next Steve Jobs . . . Every good leader needs plenty of good followers.

~ Emma, The Eccentric Assistant

Spotlight: Leo the CEO

Leo Martinez doesn't look like a CEO. He wears a hoodie to the pub and his iPhone isn't in a case. Now and then, he pulls it out and shoots off a message or two with a murmured apology before shifting his intense focus back to the conversation at hand. But looks are deceiving.

At 25 years young, Leo is both a millennial and one of the freelance elite—and executive of a wildly successful international apparel company, Kommon Thread, which moves thousands of units a day.

"The notion I never agreed with was the exchange of time for money," he says.

> "I think I always agreed in my head more with an exchange of 'meeting a demand in exchange for money.' So if the demand's there, I can meet it, and I request money in exchange for that."

In many ways, Leo is the embodiment of the freelance economy. His business operates on-demand, connecting clients who need custom apparel with a supply chain that provides the raw materials, design, and know-how to create that apparel. It operates with as much confidentiality as is required by the client, so reselling the apparel under another brand is never an issue. Best of all, his staff is entirely outsourced.

Leo seems to be ingrained with the entrepreneurial spirit. He spent his early childhood in Mexico, where he says "everyone sells things" to get by. There, he learned early on that running a successful business isn't about knowing all the best marketing gimmicks or having enough capital; it's about finding out what people need and selling it to them for a profit.

Leo is actually unique in that he's never needed a full-time job. In fact, his current 40-hour-a-week job at a marketing company is virtually voluntary. What free time he has left he spends advocating for the homeless and working on solutions to provide opportunity.

To illustrate this idea, Leo explained his first business, a "bookstore" he started in the ninth grade. He noticed that his peers were throwing out their books at the end of the year, the same books that students bought new from Barnes & Noble the next year, and everyone was complaining about how much it cost to get the next set of books. In response, he decided to collect the books everyone threw out, organize the lot, then sell them to the next students for half of Barnes & Noble's price. The business was all profit and no overhead; he ended up making so much money that he was able to buy all the equipment he needed to start his own screen-printing business, which became the foundation of www.KommonThread.com

Busy as he is, Leo says he couldn't imagine doing anything else. To him, running a business has always been more of a game than a chore. Even after a recent bad luck streak—his websites were hacked by an unknown competitor shortly before our interview—he said that he sees every setback as a new challenge:

> "I take life as it comes. It's an adventure. I want to see what's around the corner."

What I like about Leo is that he never let anyone's expectations hold him back. While most people his age are battling student debt payments and struggling to find their place in an unstable job market, Leo has harnessed his passion to carve out a place for himself. His story is as much a rags to riches story as it is a reminder of the power of self-motivation.

⟦⇨ DO **THIS** / NOT **THAT** ⇦⟧

Do: Set realistic goals for yourself and your potential business.

Wherever you're starting from is going to determine how successful your business will be for the first few years. There's something to be said for "you have to have money to make money," so however long it takes you to earn that capital is something you're going to have to factor in. Don't break the bank—be reasonable with your risks, have a fallback plan, and document everything.

Don't: Take on more responsibility than you can handle.

What's true for beginning freelancers stays true for beginning employers: you don't want to take on too much. There's a learning curve to managing someone else's time in addition to your own, so you don't want to hire 20 people at once and assume that you're going to figure it out as you go along, even if you can afford it. If you absolutely must jump into the deep end, at least make sure you hire an experienced mentor who can talk you through the chaos.

Reviews, Rejection, and Redemption

CHAPTER 8

No matter what kind of freelancer you end up becoming, reviews are something you're going to have to live with. Everyone everywhere gets reviewed nowadays: Yelp has become the new Yellow Pages for business, Amazon reviews can make or break a product, and a good LinkedIn recommendation can be what gets you your dream job. For contractors, your digital reputation is more than just a necessary evil—it's your livelihood. Tarnish it, and you might not be able to secure your next client, which means that cash flow is going to take a dip quickly.

Not that you should live in fear. Reviews can be a great way to take the temperature of your general work performance, and as long as you don't let the scale tip too far the wrong way, it's mostly benefit. In this chapter, you'll find how to use reviews to your advantage, and what you can do to manage your online reputation (without finding a service to do it for you).

Garnering Reviews

Scary as reviews are, it's better to have them than to not. It's like disabling the comments on a YouTube video: it's tempting, but there's something suspicious about a user that refuses to collect anyone's opinion.

It's also the first way potential clients/customers vet you. It stands to reason that a client would give *at least* as much scrutiny to a freelancer as they would to massage chairs on Amazon, in their hunt for the best possible product. Check the price, skim the competition, and once the search is narrowed, weigh the reviews. If there aren't any, move on.

So, Step 1: Make sure you're visible. The way you do this depends on your business, but the easiest way to start is to ask your most recent clients to write you a few words on LinkedIn. If most of your clients are by referral, LinkedIn is going to be the primary face of your digital reputation.

From there, take a look at your portfolio. Has anything you've done recently been in the public eye? Maybe you designed the logo for a T-shirt that's now selling on Amazon. Screenshot the reviews that love your design and add those to your website. Maybe it's time you start a blog. In any case, be sure that the Internet knows who you are and keep track of how it responds.

If you're just getting started, this is another way that on-demand platforms can benefit you. Aspiring writers on Upwork can charge less for their services and gather reputation from incoming client reviews. Likewise, a jewelry business can test out an Etsy page instead of using a Weebly shop.

When you're first getting acquainted with your digital reputation, you might also want to take the time to Google yourself. Even if your life is squeaky clean, other people with your name might not be. One *Forbes* article suggests going as far as reserving a Google profile, email address, and domain in your name to prevent it from being used by imposters.[62] Clear your history and search your name: if the first five pages of returned results look reputable, you're good to go. If not, fixing that (by adding new, more favorable pages on the Web) should be at the top of your list.

Learning from Less Favorable Reviews

If any feedback isn't quite what you expected, resist the urge to dismiss it outright. It's easy to say someone is "too sensitive," or "just doesn't understand my process." Remember, like there's truth in every joke, there's truth in all disgruntled feedback.

Say you get a review that says you were the worst handyman they had ever hired. Sure, you probably weren't the worst, really—but there was something you did that made them say that! Take a deep breath and really reflect on all feedback you receive.

If anything, you can keep it in mind going into the next job. Maybe you can better align expectations up front. Regardless, the important thing is not to take it personally. Rejection is a part of the freelance world; not every business relationship is going to work out.

---

[62] Wilkinson, S. (2014, March 14). "From Mocking to Hacking: How to Protect Your Digital Reputation." *Forbes.* Retrieved from http://www.forbes.com/sites/85broads/2014/03/14/from-mocking-to-hacking-how-to-protect-your-digital-reputation/#7633c3f828fe

Of course, it is possible that your client was crazy. For that, you can vent on websites like http://clientsfromhell.net. However, as a great blog on Groove HQ put it, there's a difference between challenging customers and bad customers. Their argument is that a challenging customer alerts you to problems within a product that most customers don't bother to tell you about—the survey they cite says that for every one complaint, 26 customers have kept silent about the same problem—while a bad customer is one who threatens, makes unreasonable demands, and who generally "makes your life hell."[63]

In this case, clients are just like customers. If the negative feedback seems earnest, give it a second thought. If you want to engage with the client and see if you might repair the relationship, respond nondefensively, and be sure to take the conversation into a private space (like email) as quickly as possible. But if the feedback comes from a client like this, take it with a grain of salt:

Me: I've finished uploading the article!

Client: Super. In the future, do you mind uploading images to go along with the articles?

Me: Do you mean images that can be published along with the article or photos for your personal reference? I'm happy to do either, provided you have a photo-subscription account like Shutterstock. In any case, we would need to acquire permission for whatever image you'd like to use. Let me know what you'd like to do!

Client: Use google and submit search request for photos that are available for unrestricted usage. PS: <u>Please don't be condescending.</u> It's a disgusting trait on a woman.

[63] Markidan, L. (2014, November 18). "Why It's OK to Fire Your Bad Customers." GrooveHQ. Retrieved from https://www.groovehq.com/support/how-to-fire-a-bad-customer

Redeeming Yourself After a Slump

According to *Forbes*, it takes roughly five positive interactions to make up for one negative one. Roughly, that means for every negative review, you should work to bring in five better ones.[64] Double your efforts to improve, fill tickets, and bring on the praise.

On the other hand, a string of negative reviews may be an indicator that you're starting to get tired—in other words, the first sign of burnout. If that's the case, slow down and think about whether or not your current trajectory is one you're ready for. There are hundreds of ways to freelance. Don't trap yourself in one that doesn't suit you.

The Data

How important are reviews, really?

In 2011, a professor from Harvard Business School cross-examined data from Yelp and the Washington State Department of Revenue to determine just how effective Yelp ratings were at predicting the success of a business. As it turned out, the answer is very.

A one-star rating increase on Yelp correlated to a 5% to 9% increase in revenue for independent restaurants.[65] That's enough to make or break most small establishments.

[64] DeMers, J. (2014, September 9). "How Negative Online Company Reviews Can Impact Your Business and Recruiting." *Forbes.* Retrieved April 17, 2016 from http://www.forbes.com/sites/jaysondemers/2014/09/09/how-negative-online-company-reviews-can-impact-your-business-and-recruiting/#71a239089354

[65] Luca, M. (2011, October 4). "Reviews, Reputation, and Revenue: The Case of Yelp.com." Harvard Business School. Retrieved from http://hbswk.hbs.edu/item/reviews-reputation-and-revenue-the-case-of-yelp-com

If anything, it proves that reviews do play a large part in this new interconnected marketplace, particularly for businesses selling physical goods.

On the other hand, there's a real problem with negativity bias. It's human nature that negative experiences stick out more than positive ones, which means people who had a difficult experience with something are much more likely to make their feelings known via reviews than people who had a pleasant or average experience.

For instance, *Forbes* describes a survey carried out by Workplace Dynamics regarding the correlation between negative feedback on the employer-reviewing website Glassdoor and the overall employee satisfaction at those companies: after comparing surveys they had done with 406 companies to the corresponding Glassdoor ratings, the survey found almost no consistency between the two sources. They write: "We found that there was virtually no correlation—the overall Glassdoor star rating was a very poor indicator of what it is really like to work at a company."[66]

So, as much as we trust reviews, the fact is that they may not be as accurate as we think they are. Not that that's stopping us. The 2015 Internet Trends survey says that the number of user-generated reviews across websites like Airbnb increased 140% from 2014 to 2015,[67] and I'll bet that number is only going to get higher. Flawed or not, it's a system that's here to stay. The younger the decision maker, the higher likelihood they will choose based on online reviews. Case in point, the updated 2017 Internet Trends reports that 34% of millennials choose a medical provider based on online reviews, four times the number of baby boomers (at 8%) who do so.

[66] DeMers, J. (2014, September 9). "How Negative Online Company Reviews Can Impact Your Business and Recruiting." *Forbes*. Retrieved from http://www.forbes.com/sites/jaysondemers/2014/09/09/how-negative-online-company-reviews -can-impact-your-business-and-recruiting/#71a239089354
[67] Meeker, M. (2015, May 27). "America's Evolving Work Environment." *Internet Trends 2015—Code Conference*, KPCB, Kleiner Perkins Coufield & Byers, 126.

The Takeaway

The best thing a freelancer can do is be proactive. If the platform allows it, respond to all reviews publicly—the good, bad, and even ugly.

Be gracious and publicly thank those that give you kudos, and be courteous and professional to those reviews that aren't so glowy.

Keep your reviews positive by doing your best work, and course correct when you find yourself marked with criticism. And if you ever find yourself slipping, remember that redemption is always possible.

Spotlight: Poo~Pourri

Poo~Pourri is toilet spray. You spray it into the toilet before you sit down so your business doesn't stink. Marketing that sounds like an advertiser's worst nightmare, but astoundingly, Poo~Pourri was profitable within two months of production, growing word-of-mouth as people purchased the product from shops and boutiques and then the Internet.[68] Their hilarious taglines, coupled with a surprisingly effective product, easily garnered prestige across social media.

What's really impressive is how well Poo~Pourri was able to harness their positive feedback. The momentum from their initial sales grew their Facebook following, expanding across other social networks like Twitter, Pinterest, and Instagram.

Customers who discovered the product through these sites would be directed to Amazon for a purchase; happy customers there created a steady stream of positive reviews that continued to increase their visibility. When they dropped their first ever advertisement, "Girls Don't Poop," these happy and dedicated followers shared the ad, and it went viral. It was 2013's fifth most viewed ad on YouTube.[69]

[68] Babich, E. (2013, May 3). "Suzy Batiz Turns Foul Odors into Sweet Smell of Success." *BizJournals*. Retrieved from http://www.bizjournals.com/dallas/print-edition/2013/05/03/whats-that-smell-money.html?page=all
[69] Nudd, T. (2013, December 11). "The 10 Most Watched Ads on YouTube in 2013: These Supervirals Earned Your Attention Instead of Just Paying for It." Adweek. Retrieved from http://www.adweek.com/news-gallery/advertising-branding /10-most-watched-ads-youtube-2013-154423#poopourricom-girls-dont-poop-5

Naturally, Poo~Pourri's success is due as much to great branding as it is to visible reviews. Founder Suzy Batiz is clearly someone who knows what product she's selling. Suzy says she sold out at her first trade show by wheeling in an actual toilet filled with lemons to put on display;[70] a 2014 article by *Bizwomen* features a picture of Batiz seated on a porcelain throne, grinning wildly at the camera.[71]

> Clearly, it takes someone with guts and a great sense of humor about themselves to put together a company that capitalizes on bathroom odor.

But the fascinating part is just how much their Amazon reviews may have helped launch them into fame. In the YouTube ad, they declared that over 1,000 reviews gave the product 4.8 out of 5 stars, statistics that fly in the face of the negativity bias that means that most products will never maintain a nearly 5-star rating.[72] When you hear those kinds of numbers, you can't help but pay attention.

Following the ad, the Facebook fanbase grew by 70% within the first year and continued to skyrocket, with audiences on their other social media pages following suit.[73] Not only did it dramatically expand their reach, it brought in paying customers. According to a 2016 CNBC feature, the company suddenly had $4 million in back orders after the surge in

[70] Urry, K. (2015, March 9). "Nothing but Brilliant: Poo~Pourri Marketing." Tint Up. Retrieved from http://www.tintup.com/blog/nothing-brilliant-poopourri-marketing/

[71] Ryan, M. (2014, June 18). "When Your Business Revolves Around Poo, Marketing is Tricky. Here's How Suzy Batiz Made It Go Viral." *BizWomen*. Retrieved from http://www.bizjournals.com/bizwomen/news/profiles-strategies/2014/06/how-suzy-batiz-marketed-the-crap-out-of-a-taboo.html?page=all

[72] Ackerman, J. (Director). (2013). *Girls Don't Poop - PooPourri.com*. USA: YouTube. https://www.youtube.com/watch?v=ZKLnhuzh9uY

[73] Raghupathi, R. (2013, November 19). "20 Million Views Later, How Poo~Pourri Made a Splash on Social Media." Social Media Today. Retrieved from http://www.socialmediatoday.com/content/20-million-views-later-how-poopourri-made-splash-social-media

popularity, forcing Batiz to contact their manufacturer's CEO to solve major production delays. Who said you can't have too much of a good thing?

There's even a touch of redemption in this story. Before inventing Poo~Pourri, founder Batiz went through not one, but two bankruptcies.[74] No doubt the credit damage was immense—its own kind of review, unfortunately—but Batiz had obviously learned from her failures and worked to make sure that this time she would come out on top. If the current 58,000 YouTube subscribers and 7,000 Amazon reviews (still at 4.8 stars) are any indication, it was all worth it.

The lesson here is simple:
if you deliver quality work, stay true to
your message, and stand out from the
crowd, customers will respond. And if
you have a way to harness that response,
amazing things can happen.

If it can happen for toilet spray,
it can happen for you.

---

[74] Wells, J. (2016, January 26). "A Business That Doesn't Stink: Solving Poo Odor." CNBC. Retrieved from http://www.cnbc.com/2016/01/26/a-business-that-doesnt-stink-solving-poo-odor.html

⟦⇨ DO **THIS** / NOT **THAT** ⇦⟧

Do:: Exceed expectations on any service where you're being reviewed (and even when you're not).

It's impossible to say whether or not this project is the one that's going to be on your digital record. Always do your best work for the sake of doing so, and assume that feedback will follow. If it doesn't happen this time, or the next time, it may happen when you least expect it. Who knows? It could be a year before your client stumbles on your page again and decides to leave some words of appreciation.

Don't: Forget to ask for feedback.

Because reviews can be scary business, many freelancers shy away from asking for them. Don't. Reach out to the clients you've served—as soon after the job is finished as possible—and ask for a testimonial. You can send a request through LinkedIn, ask them to write a Yelp review, or just request an emailed quote for your website. As a caveat, never try to force clients to give positive feedback. Often, when you try to drag a good review out of people you think will speak highly of you, it backfires, and the recommendation comes across as forced, fake, or, worse, milquetoast.

CHAPTER 9

Ethics in the Gig Economy

With globalization, cultural differences, generational evolution, and public political discord, ethics are (and will continue to be) fungible. We all temper our "that's not fair!" child-like tantrums with the reality that any one of us, if given the opportunity, would likely shift the balance of power to benefit ourselves or our families. Ethical practices are not about "fairness," per se, but rather about what lets us all sleep well at night. That is probably one of the main reasons you are reading this book: to learn how to successfully make a living in the new economy . . . in a way that feels *right* to you!

Like everything else in the modern world, freelance ethics can be a bit ill-defined. To date, there are no across-the-board rules or standards for independent contractors interacting with clients, and very few laws outlining how clients can (or should) treat a contract-based workforce.

Just because there are no Commandments for freelancing, however, doesn't mean there's nothing to be gained from ethical conduct. In fact, there are benefits to outlining your own professional ethics—especially at the beginning.

Before getting into that, let's establish what I mean by ethics. So far, my favorite definition comes from *Fortune's* article on ethics and freelancing: "principles or a code of conduct [that] give professionals a chance to anticipate and rehearse for situations and conflict."[75] This interpretation bypasses the usual moral undertones and addresses the real benefit to outlining principles: getting everyone on the same page.

Ethics Smooth Relationships

The truth is, you never know when meeting a client how the relationship is going to progress. Just as in dating, most people put their best foot forward in the networking phase, put on their best face during the honeymoon phase, and then (often accidentally) reveal themselves when the proverbial shit hits the fan. You don't want to be knee-deep in a project when your new client starts demanding you cut corners to make a deadline, especially when you're a person who can't bear anything you've worked on to be less than polished perfection. If you know that about yourself at the outset, you're less likely to get into business with someone who emphasizes speed over quality, avoiding inevitable fallout and—in the worst case—refused payment.

Ethics Remind You That You're Not a Desperate Drone

Although it can be great for clients to know the kind of person they're hiring, sometimes a code of ethics is more for you than them. Especially when you're working toward stability, it can be tempting to take a contract that otherwise violates your standards.

[75] Elmer, V. (2014, May 30). "Why Freelancers Need a Code of Ethics." *Fortune*. Retrieved from http://fortune.com/2014/05/30/why-freelancers-need-a-code-of-ethics/

Case in point: the number of questionable Upwork postings from people who want others to write their essays for them.

It's easy for a successful writer to say, "Are you kidding? I'm not doing that." But after four months of inconsistent work and falling just short of making a credit card payment, $200 for an hour of work churning out papers for a college student can start to sound tempting.

Hopefully, you'll never be in that position. Regardless, clearly outlining your own values at the beginning of the process—before desperation strikes—can help remind you when that day comes that you're better than the dark side of the Internet (or wherever that blood money is coming from).

Never Assume Anything

Even if a new client seems forthcoming at the start, they may be an entirely different person by the end of the contract. The only thing you can ever be certain of is your own standards. In short, it's your job to make sure potential clients know the person you are, and the best way to do that is with a clear-cut system of ethics, or at least a list of "Will Do / Won't Do." That way, should a client ever ask you to do anything in conflict with that system, you have cause to decline.

Your "clear expectations" don't have to be a long list (and it's best if they're not). Just a few sentences at the end of a client agreement stating that your work is your own and you pride yourself on quality—if that's your thing—is probably enough. Having strict expectations for yourself and others may scare away some potential new business.

Of course, when you're new to freelancing, you can't always be too picky. Once you have a few successes behind you, however, being choosy is to your benefit.

The best thing you can do is frame it as a win for the client. Really, any professional should want to work with people who hold themselves to a higher standard. As long as the wording is professional and brief, including some statement of ethics may end up a surprise competitive advantage in the on-demand economy.

Ethics to Consider

IIIIIIIIIIIIIIIIIIIIIIIIIIIIIIIIIIIIIIIIIIIIIIIIIIIIIIIIIIIIIIIIIIIIIIIIIIIIIIIIIIIIIIII

Not sure where to start? Though there might be a place for gray-area behavior in some types of freelancing, I believe that there are common standards that we as freelancers can abide by, most of which should be common sense. Don't cheat your clients; don't steal others' work. I'm sure we can all agree on that!

To come up with some baseline standards, I looked through the Code of Ethics currently used by the Society of Professional Journalists and then developed my own set of ideals that all freelancers can build on:

As a freelancer, I will . . .

Universal

☑ Be transparent, even if the work is not. I treat all work as if my real name and face will be plastered right next to it.

☑ Think through the process and set up checkpoints in advance for the project at hand. I communicate my proposed process to the client before beginning.

☑ Ask questions. I don't make any assumptions.

☑ Take responsibility for communicating clearly (from the start) and getting input up-front. I ensure the quality of my end product.

☑ Underpromise and overdeliver. I keep the agreements I make.

☑ Never plagiarize. I fully own all of the work that I create.

☑ Acknowledge mistakes. I make corrections promptly and prominently.

☑ Abide by the Golden Rule. I treat others as I wish to be treated.

I am a millennial, a recent college graduate, and, for the most part, I'm broke. That's a combination of factors that made me just desperate enough to clean toilets and run errands for six months while I got my writing career—more or less—off the ground; fortunately though, I can say I never did anything truly shady during my scrape through the bottom of the barrel. Do I know people that did? Absolutely.

Morally Ambiguous Job #1: Fake Amazon Reviews

My fellow English major, who we'll call Rachel, also had a hard time getting jobs right out of school. I suggested she try Upwork, and she ended up getting a long-term straight away. I chalked it up to good luck, until she finally confided in me that what she was actually doing was leaving rave reviews on Amazon products she knew nothing about. She said her client would send her a list of the product's stellar attributes, which she would then reword with pizzazz and post under a few fake profiles, then bill for the hours worked. It was easy, the money was good, but . . . if it's not illegal, then it's at least heavily frowned upon. Rachel did feel uncomfortable doing this, though not enough to stop, until one day her client suddenly said she should delete the extra profiles and disappeared.

Morally Ambiguous Job #2: Writing "News" Stories

Have you ever clicked on an article advertised at the bottom of another article that then took you to a website that wasn't the website you were on, where the article turned out to be for some kind of diet pill you're pretty sure is a parasite? Well, I had a friend who wrote those. We'll call him Steve. When I first met Steve, he was a middleman for a shipping company, then suddenly he was writing these "articles" for a Russian guy who paid obscenely well—when he paid him. The last time I saw Steve, he was waiting on $3,000 from the mysterious Russian after calling him daily for two weeks, leaving him so low on money he ran out of gas in the middle of the road and had to have his car towed back to his apartment. I assume the moral of this story is if you write shady articles for a shady Russian guy, you're going to run out of gas.

Basically, I've learned there's something to be said for maintaining a moral compass, even in the wild world of online contracting.

~ Emma, The Eccentric Assistant

Navigating from "In the App" to "Out on My Own"

☑ Be aware of the "Terms and Conditions" of every app or site I work through, and keep up with new T&C changes. Outside the app world, I use formal, signed proposals, agreements, milestone approvals, and/or contracts.

☑ Maintain my rights. I only transfer the copyright to my work (in writing) after final payment has been made.

☑ Request feedback. I ask clients to review my work.

Naturally, your personal guidelines will grow based on the type of freelancer you are and the experiences you have. Also, be flexible, both with yourself and others. No one's perfect.

The Data

One clear breakdown of ethics, for both sides, is not being paid. On the client side, it can be a result of poor budgeting, difficulty with communication, or, in rare cases, truly deceitful business practices. On the contractor's side, not being paid could mean failing to deliver on promises, shoddy workmanship, failure to communicate effectively, or the inability to pick up on early warning signs that this was not a client to be relied on.

Whatever the reason, not getting paid for a project is devastating. And, unfortunately, it happens more than it should. A New York -based study of self-employed people found that 35% of them were paid late at least once during the preceding year, while 14% did work for clients who never paid at all. The total wages lost over 12 months in New York State alone were more than $3 billion.[76] That is a terrifying number.

The Freelancers Union conducted a similar survey regarding payment difficulties among freelancers in 2014.[77] Here are just a handful of their findings:

1 in every 2 freelancers had trouble getting paid in 2014.

71% cited trouble collecting payment at some point in their career.

81% of those who had payment trouble in 2014 said they were paid late.

34% cited instances of not being paid at all.

Freelancers lost an average of **$5,968** in unpaid income in 2014, detracting **13%** of the average respondent's annual income.

Late and nonpayment occurs at high rates across all industries and types of work.

If you take anything from those numbers, it's that nonpayment is a real danger for freelancers, and it's something that you're going to have to guard against every way that you can.

Knowing your values and communicating them to your client at the start, making sure you sign a clear contract, and having a plan for when things go south are all steps that will protect you

[76] Fisher, A. (2013, March 29). "How to Get Paid, Not Played." *Fortune*. Retrieved from http://fortune.com/2013/03/29/a-freelance-dilemma-how-to-get-paid-not-played/
[77] Horowitz, S. (2015). "The Costs of Nonpayment: A Study of Nonpayment and Late Payment in the Freelance Workforce. Freelancers Union." Retrieved from https://fu-web-storage-prod.s3.amazonaws.com/content/advocacy/uploads/resources/FU_NonpaymentReport_r3.pdf

from becoming part of these statistics. Also, keep copies of all communication between you and your client: letters, emails, texts, and voice messages are all essential documentation when facing a dispute down the line. (Also, another reason to stay on your best behavior.)

For those specializing in creative work, withhold the copyright on all work until a final payment is made. It's far more threatening to sue for copyright than to try to take someone to small claims court; copyright suits are far more arduous, and even difficult clients will likely settle than fight them.

I also put in my contracts that I reserve the right to use the work in my portfolio, even after the copyright has transferred to the client, but decide for yourself how much you want to press your luck.

The Takeaway

While we don't yet have a universal Freelancer Code of Ethics, defining your own standard of conduct can put you in a better position to judge potential clients and provide a good foundation for the freelancer-client relationships you choose to develop.

The freelance economy can only survive if all its participants behave ethically—and although you can't guarantee that everyone you work with is going to be professional, having standards for yourself brings the rest one step closer to this ideal.

[⇨ DO **THIS** / NOT **THAT** ⇦]

Do: Take time to outline your "Will Do / Won't Do" list before taking on any big jobs.

Even if you don't have rigid ethical boundaries, everyone has things that they will and won't do when they're in a stable position. It's important that you establish this for yourself before delving too deep into the freelancing world, where it's easy to lose yourself in the pursuit of payday.

Don't: Break too many of your own rules.

In times of desperation, it's tempting to take jobs that you'd normally resist. However, every job you take moves your career in a certain direction, and later you might regret how those desperate decisions reflect on your character. If things get difficult, try putting your statement of ethics somewhere you can see it. You'll thank yourself later on.

CHAPTER 10 › Living in the Future

Everything in our lives is being automated, personalized, and optimized, thanks to our robot overlords—well, technically, the emergence of artificial intelligence, otherwise known as "machine learning." It's what drives your continued scrolling down your feed in social media until you lose track of time. AI determines which advertisements are stitched into that facebook feed—ones you'll click on. Search online, and the robots lead you to pay for a test that speaks to how your genetic makeup influences your choice of diet. Stitch fix uses a computer-generated model to become your customized online personal stylist. Google Calendar is now my external brain that keeps track of everything, from birthdays to my daughter's school schedule to when airline tickets are cheapest. If you spoke to Amazon Echo or Google in your home this last year, you have AI to thank, as Google machine learning voice recognition reached the 95% level of human word accuracy for the first time ever in 2017.[78]

And lest you think our robot overlords have figured everything out, turns out they still have some explaining to do. Like in 2017, when an AI-based decision engine sold phone case designs on Amazon based on what was trending in stock image searches. The results were disastrously comic and included an old man in a diaper, a cheese wheel on some sexy abs, and heroin in a spoon.

---

[78] Meeker, M. (2017, May) "Internet Trends Report." Kleiner Perkins Caufield & Byers. Retrieved from http://www.kpcb.com/internet-trends

Whatever help we need in the modern world, there's an app for that. Adults spend over three hours a day consuming digital media on their mobile device, up from under one hour just five years ago.

On the flip side of all this technology candy is the day-after Halloween hangover. Is my job at risk? The automation, machine, and AI anxiety is understandable. A widely mentioned Oxford study made it seem that nearly half of all jobs in the US were at risk of being automated by 2033. How worried should we be?

The Robopocalypse Is Not Happening

IIIIIIIIIIIIIIIIIIIIIIIIIIIIIIIIIIIIIIIIIIIIIIIIIIIIIIIIIIIIIIIIII

Is it too much to think of the workforce changing fundamentally into a different animal, part driven by AI, but mostly driven by the humans using AI behind smartphones?

As a fan of Elon Musk, I pay attention to when he and other tech titans warn of a jobless future. They go as far as to argue for a social safety net in the form of a basic income once the robots take all the paid jobs.

The thing is, there isn't much out there to show that we are on that inevitable path.

James Surowieki writes in *The Great Tech Panic: Robots Won't Take All Our Jobs* that

"Since automation allows companies to produce more with fewer people, a great wave of automation should drive higher productivity growth. Yet, in reality, productivity gains over the past decade have been, by historical standards, dismally low. Back in the heyday of the US economy, from 1947 to 1973, labor productivity grew at an average pace of nearly 3 percent a year. Since 2007, it has grown at a rate of around 1.2 percent, the slowest pace in any period since World War II. And over the past two years, productivity has grown at a mere 0.6 percent— the very years when anxiety about automation has spiked. That's simply not what you'd see if efficient robots were replacing inefficient humans en masse."[79]

Surowieki actually points to China being at the root of our job woes, not automation, as 2.4 million jobs have disappeared just in 1999–2011 due to massive trade deficits, driven by manufacturing (and all our Amazon purchases!).

Further, he argues that embracing AI as a nation "broadly defined, could lift annual GDP growth in the US by two points (to 4.6 percent). A growth rate like that would make it easy to deal with the cost of things like Social Security and Medicare and the rising price of health care. It would lead to broader wage growth. And while it would complicate the issue of how to divide the economic pie, it's always easier to divide a growing pie than a shrinking one."

With that, I'm going to take a deep humanizing breath, relax, and ask for my robot bartender to make me a cocktail.

[79] Surowieki, J (2017, Aug) "The Great Tech Panic: Robots Won't Take All Our Jobs." *Wired*. Retrieved from https://www.wired.com/2017/08/robots-will-not-take-your-job/

Spotlight: Trust as Currency

I recently spoke to Dr. Norah Dunbar, a featured "What the Research Says" contributor in *Sell Local, Think Global*, on what the future of work holds for us all. Dr. Norah Dunbar is a well respected professor, researcher, and Chair of Communication at the University of California, Santa Barbara.

NORAH DUNBAR, PHD

We both agreed that trust underpins the new working world order. That is one reason reviews get an entire chapter in this book. Why is trust so important to understand and harness? I'll let her take it away in her own words:

Establishing Trust in the Gig Economy
Norah Dunbar, PhD

What is trust? Social scientists from a variety of fields have been tackling this issue for many years and have converged on the idea that trust comes from two sources:

(1) An interdependence with another person; and
(2) a willingness to make yourself vulnerable to that person.

Interdependence means that neither partner can achieve their goals without the help of the other partner. You rely on that person and come to have certain expectations about them. As trust develops, you begin to believe that other people will value the relationship more than their own goals. That's where vulnerability comes in. In a trusting relationship, you are willing to take risks. You "put your neck out" for people whom you trust and expect they will do the same for you. When you work with someone for many years, like many employees do when they work for the same company for a long time, you learn who can be counted on and who cannot. Who has your back? Who will support you in a crisis? Who will help you succeed in achieving your goals? Who will pitch in and go the extra mile when they are needed?

In the gig economy, trust can be more difficult to establish because people are not as dependent on one another as they are when they work together for the same company. Their relationships are more short-term, and they don't have well-established expectations for the future. You might hire a web designer to spruce up your company webpage one time and then hire someone else the next time.

People don't have the same level of commitment or trust with one another in short-term gigs. How can you establish trust in this situation?

Generally, trust is developed slowly over time, but sometimes you can create what researchers call "swift trust" by reducing uncertainty about your future behavior, creating expectations for what you will do next, and communicating clearly about your role. Even virtual teams who never meet face-to-face can establish swift trust if they communicate well. Think about ways to create expectations for the future. Always follow through on your promises to create the sense that someone can rely on you again. Take risks to show that you are willing to trust others, and create a sense of vulnerability by putting other people's goals ahead of your own.

Suggested reading about the science of trust:

DeSteno, D. (2014). *The Truth About Trust: How It Determines Success in Life, Love, Learning, and More.* Penguin.

Gottman, J. M. (2011). *The Science of Trust: Emotional Attunement for Couples.* W. W Norton & Company.

Rousseau, D. M., S. B., Sitkin, R. S., Burt, and C. Camerer, (1998). "Not So Different After All: A Cross-Discipline View of Trust." *The Academy of Management Review*, 23(3), 393–404.

Simpson, J. A. (2007). "Psychological Foundations of Trust." *Current Directions in Psychological Science*, 16(5), 264–268.

Wildman, J. L., M. L., Shuffler, E. H., Lazzara, S. M., Fiore, C. S., Burke, E., Salas, and S. Garven, (2012). "Trust Development in Swift Starting Action Teams: A Multilevel Framework." *Group & Organization Management*, 37(2), 137–170.

So, Where to Go from Here? As Easy as 1-2-3

First, take stock of your skill set by understanding your Unique Value Proposition (remember that from Chapter 3?). Bonus! You can write it all out in the worksheets provided in the appendix. I'll also help you with the most updated, full-sized toolkit at www.chunkofchange.com/gigisup

Second, start to use some of the platforms in Chapter 2 yourself. Get to know what it is to go paddleboarding with an Airbnb experience host like myself or an experience close by. Or hire someone for a small task on any of the platforms we speak about in Chapter 2.

Third, and most importantly, work on that elusive skill that asks others to review you to highlight those *-ests* (Review Chapter 8). In the future of work, trust is underpinning that leads to getting the job—er, gig—or not.

You are worth it. I'm here for you. Do not go at it alone. We are a community. Thanks for reading and keep in touch!

Let's continue the conversation:

- linkedin.com/in/olgamizrahi
- @olgamizrahi
- @chunkofchange

APPENDIX

What Makes You Different?

||||||||||||||||||||||||||||||||||||||||||||||||||||||||||||||||||

A value proposition is an inherent promise of benefit that you give your clients, customers, or business partners. That value is usually measured in terms of "benefit minus cost." Of course, a large part of determining value lies in comparing the alternatives.

A Unique Value Proposition communicates your unique contribution and/or services/products that you are able to provide to the market—in a way that is different from your competitors.

It's paramount to communicate the *unique* part of the UVP, answering the "Why should someone choose you in particular?" and "What makes you different?" questions. Start by brainstorming, as a team with your most trusted partners, asking, "Who am I, if I were a company of one?" It's a big feat to be able to clearly and concisely answer the question. There are several ways to look at it though. You can provide several kinds of definitions:

• A technical definition, which outlines the specific services
  you're able to provide
• A character definition, which says something about the
personality of your group of people
• A market map definition, which identifies where you fall within
  your group of competitors

☞ If You Provide a Product
Your Unique Value Proposition might consist of

- A high perceived value;
- Unique packaging;
- Standout design;
- Ease of use; or
- The ability to fill a need better than competing products.

☞ If You Provide a Service
You might be different because of

- Faster response time;
- The ability to offer more for less;
- A high level of expertise;
- The perception that you bring more to the table;
  or
- The ability to time the service offering that you
  have with a particular need.

☞ If You Provide Something Else
Even if you're not selling a product or service (as is the case with many nonprofit organizations), you still have to tell people what unique value they'll get for their money, which may include

- A "fit" with a particular value system (i.e. it elicits an emotion);
- Personal identification with an issue (i.e. it strikes a chord);
- Alleviation of an anxiety (i.e. it quells a negative feeling); or
- Some sort of tangible incentive (e.g. a gift with donation).

Now It's Your Turn
(What Makes You Different?)

||||||||||||||||||||||||||||||||||||||||||||||||||||||||||||||||||||||

1. If my friends were to describe me to someone new, the top three words they would use would be . . .

   _____

2. The top three ways I help people are . . .

   _____

3. The top three things I'm the very best at are . . .

   _____

4. One thing I can offer the world that other people are unwilling or unable to provide is . . .

   _____

5. The main thing that makes me different from other people is . . .

   _____

6. The number one benefit of being my friend is . . .

   _____

I am a (1) person, who gives the world (2). I excel at (3) and am proud to offer (4). I stand apart from others because I am (5). For these reasons and more, I am known as a person who is valued by others because I am (6).

Linking Benefits Worksheet

Why Am I Choosing You?

It won't really matter if you're super awesome if no one knows it. How are you going to shout your irresistibleness from the rooftops? The things that make you awesome, those UVP points, are features of you. What the person that chooses you wants to understand clearly is how that will benefit them. Be as specific and succinct as possible.

Fill out a few of these to get the hang of it:

I'm awesome because

_____ &

That benefits you by

_____.

I'm awesome because

_____ &

That benefits you by

_____.

I'm awesome because

_____ &

That benefits you by

_____ .

Examples:

I'm awesome because
I am the best at unearthing your personal brand. &
That benefits you by
getting hired by those that are the best fit for you.

I'm awesome because
I am featured in *Fast Company, Inc.* and *Forbes.* &
That benefits you by
touting that credibility to your target market
when you hire me to speak.

I'm awesome because
my newest digital marketing class is offered
by the University of California, Irvine. &
That benefits you by
getting innovative marketing knowledge to your
team when you hire me to teach them.

Acknowledgments

||||||||||||||||||||||||||||||||||||||||||||||||||||||||||||||||||||||||||

Thank you to my students/muses in all things, including you, dear reader, and to all the organizations that I'm privileged to speak to and the topics I'm honored to present: Digital Marketing, Personal Branding, Transmedia Branding Through Storytelling at UCI, and beyond. You all keep me learning, every day.

My clients, colleagues, and collaborators are the inspiration and perspiration behind bringing the wisdom I've earned to print. I sincerely thank Kimberly Grietzer, Tom Jacobsen, Mark Chapman, Dimple Thakkar, Steve Kinney, Katie Covell, William Brandon, Patricia Handschiegel, Daniel Tepke, and my number one proofreader and supporter, Avery Mizrahi.

Special thanks to Emma Austin, Sarah Daniels, Artin Aghamalian, Leo Martinez, and Liya Swift for lending your voices to the conversation. Dr. Norah Dunbar graciously gave her social research lens, and I am indebted to her. Norah, thank you for continuing to cross over from academia to add to the work of laymen.

Jamie Ponchak has been my graphic enabler at ohso! design for the past thirteen years, and the fabulous modern design of this book is thanks to her. Jamie, I am grateful for you in my work life and beyond.

Jim Hanson always gets a special acknowledgment for holding down the fort and meeting the demands of our clients with ever-changing technology.

A big thank you for the love and support from my husband, Geoff, and his wonderful family (Sherry, Al, Patti, Deanna, Tim, Doug, the Houses, and Garrisons); my Polish family (Skowronscy!); the Polish

Posse: Bartek, Susie, Ella, and Adam Korsak and Monica and Sam Tye in particular, who are all wind beneath my wings.

A special shout out to all the boards I've served on, without whom I wouldn't have been introduced to some of the great thought leaders who inspired me to write, like Brian Solis, Seth Godin, Chris Brogan, David Merman Scott, and James Altucher, and, even more importantly, the fabulous women who continue to inspire me: Judie Vivian and Pat Bramhall, I'm looking at you!

Thank you to the readers and commenters at *The Long Beach Post* and ChunkofChange.com. You inspire me to do my best work.

Finally, a big thank you to the team at Greenleaf Book Group—it's so refreshing to communicate with a publisher that gets it!

And a big heartfelt thanks to you all; you make me a better person and life-long learner.

Reading Group Guide

||||||||||||||||||||||||||||||||||||||||||||||||||||||||||||||||||||||||

1. How can you translate the tips in this book into your own life and work?

2. Are you currently part of the gig economy? Are the tips and advice in this book an accurate portrayal of this lifestyle for you?

3. How will a Unique Value Proposition help you stand out in the gig economy?

4. What are tools from this book that you will implement to help land your next freelance project?

5. What new on-demand app have you discovered as a result of reading this book?

6. How has reading *The Gig Is Up* changed the way you buy a product, service, or donate your time and money?

7. How has reading *The Gig Is Up* changed the way you present yourself in order to be hired?

8. Has reading *The Gig Is Up* changed the way you view new people that are coming to the table in the gig economy (i.e., on-demand workers, contract workers, freelancers)?

9. What is the most helpful piece of advice you read in this book?

10. If you're a freelancer, do you use any of the services talked about in this book? What is your experience with these freelancing services?

11. Do you use any freelancing services not mentioned in this book? Discuss any success or trouble found with any of them.

12. What made you pick up this book and learn about the gig economy? If you are already a freelancer, discuss your motivations for leaving the traditional workforce.

13. What is something you didn't now about the gig economy before reading this book?

14. If you owned your own business, what qualities would you look for in a freelancer?

15. Have your requirements and expectations changed since reading this book?

16. What is the driving force behind your decision to enter the gig economy? Discuss other factors pushing people away from traditional jobs.

17. What are some habits that, after reading this book, you feel you could work on in order to become a more successful freelancer?

18. What is hardest about being a freelancer? The most rewarding?

19. Have you ever had an ethical dilemma while on a freelance project? Explain.

20. What are your goals as a freelancer? How will you use this book to reach those goals?

21. What motivates you to complete a freelance project? How does that change when you start getting burned out? What are some of your own ways of keeping yourself from getting burned out?

Author Q&A

IIIIIIIIIIIIIIIIIIIIIIIIIIIIIIIIIIIIIIIIIIIIIIIIIIIIIIIIIIIIIIIIIIIIIIIII

Q: Were there any topics you were unable to explore in this book that you wanted to? If so, what were they?

A: The sharing economy is moving so fast that there are new web platforms and on-demand mobile apps that come up every week. With a tap of your finger you can order massages with Soothe, get your kids safely from school to the soccer field with an Uber-like app for kids called Kango, or even hail a private jet with JetSmart-er. (What?!?) It's so hard to keep track, and who knows which ones will stay relevant, or pivot into something else entirely. I hope that I am successful in giving the reader a framework to understand and evaluate the types of opportunities out there, rather than just blindly chase after the latest buzz.

Q: What was the biggest challenge you faced as you were writing this book?

A: Making sure that the easy-to-understand concepts helped the most and stayed relevant in the fast-paced on-demand economy.

Q: What is the most important concept from this book for readers looking to enter the gig economy?

A: Really understanding and embracing your Unique Value Proposition (UVP) as a foundation. Then, understanding how to communicate your UVP to those that do the choosing.

Q: You give lots of tips on staying on task. Which one(s) of these helps you the most, and do you have any helpers of your own that you didn't mention?

A: I think it is different for everyone, but do have a consciousness of the whirlwind around you and understand there are ways to harness that energy! The tools I use daily are a mix of my Google calendar (a.k.a. External brain!), a weekly at-a-glance spreadsheet, a daily board I wipe off, and ongoing strategy that looks further out. I actually provide my weekly at-a-glance one-pager for free to my fabulous readers at www.ChunkOfChange.com/gigisup.

Q: What makes your book unique from other books on the same topic?

A: Get chosen. *The Gig Is Up* offers the best boots-on-the-ground methods for success, by evolving the reader's perspective and process. Many books on the gig economy focus on letting people live out their dreams, instead of looking at the realities of what it truly takes to win in a world of increasing choice. People need to understand how to compete and how to put the best version of themselves up front and center. The goal in competing today is to not only be chosen but to move toward becoming the only choice, over and over again

How's that for a Unique Value Proposition?

Q: What do you think is the biggest reason people fail in the gig economy?

A: The same reason so many businesses fail. Either you are not really providing the benefit you think you are, are not clear enough in the benefit you provide, are not boldly stating that benefit to those doing the choosing, or are not getting the attention of enough people that pay for what you offer.

Q: Have you found that there are other benefits of freelancing over traditional jobs in terms of wage gap issues and discrimination?

A: In an ideal world, the freelance economy is meritocracy driven. That is, people are chosen based on the excellent skill set they bring or their availability in a local area, rather than their sex, race, gender identity, sexual preference, or physical limitations that aren't related to the skill needed. We see this in Lyft drivers, where according to a Sherpa study, females make up 30 percent the drivers. Compare that to less than 1 percent of New York City taxi drivers, and you start to see the power to change the workforce.

Q: Would you ever shift back to a traditional job?

A: No. Once you go gig by choice, a flexible schedule and the freedom to speak your mind without political repercussion is addicting. If you ever go back to a traditional job, you would probably make a terrible employee. ;-)

Q: What was the biggest adjustment you had to make when you became a business owner?

A: Being constantly connected 24-7 means a new skillset must be learned: boundary setting. It's too easy to be working all the time.

Q: What is the next step for you? Are you writing a new book or interested in a new business?

A: I strive to become the most helpful resource and teacher for people interested in being chosen in the gig economy or those wanting to know how to manage teams made up of freelancers. I welcome reader comments on how I could be the most supportive for them. I think we should all become a supportive community that understands how to clearly and boldly do what we do best.

Q: Who or what has been the biggest influence in achieving your goals and getting you to where you are today in your work life?

A: I am open to mentorship and people in my life who serve advisory roles. I've been blessed by many generous folks who support and help me work through my goals. I was having dinner recently with a super bright person I profile in this book. She was lamenting the lack of mentors, specifically female mentors, and I was thinking to myself, *I'm sitting right here, you just have to ask.* People have a hard time with asking. I even prompted her: "How can I best support you?" and proceeded to ask if a particular introduction with a potential client would be good for her. Her answer was "Yes! In the future . . ." It is a perspective change to allow people in your life—now—not when you have a perfect website, resume, video, and so on.

Q: At the end of your book, you speak about exporting work to China being the real threat to US jobs rather than automation. Are there any other threats to the future of the job market that you see as real concerns?

A: Yes, it all comes down to power, specifically what governments can do to support the rise of the gig worker. I think there is real power in portable benefits that free people from the worry of healthcare and retirement. If this can be figured out, you'll have a lot more people in the gig economy by choice rather than the stories of working sixty hours a week in three potentially dead-end jobs with no benefits.

Q: Do you see any changes to the gig economy happening in the future?

A: More competition, more fighting for attention, and more ways of doing things that you won't be able to live without. I love living in the future.

Q: Is freelancing as fast growing in other countries as it is here in the United States?

A: I reference the McKinsey Global Institute survey, which looked at around 8,000 respondents across the US and Europe (France, Germany, Spain, Sweden, and the UK). All the countries are seeing a sharp increase in the independants, currently estimated at 25–30 percent of the workforce.

Q: How is the international gig economy different from a domestic one?

A: In some ways, it depends a lot on mobile penetration. It may be surprising to learn that the US does not lead the world in smartphone use relative to its population; we see around 70 percent mobile penetration, whereas South Korea is at 88 percent! If you're in Brazil, you may find that only one-third of those around you are using their smartphones as fully connected to the World Wide Web. Because I view smartphone connectivity and usage as the backbone of what is fueling the new economy, you can see how this would vary country to country.

Q: What is the most common question others ask you about the gig economy, and how do you answer that question?

A: How to survive! People are incredibly concerned that their traditional jobs are disappearing, or morphing to contract positions, and they feel powerless. There are things you can do to be prepared for the changes coming and give yourself a leg up in order to get chosen! I believe the foundation ties into Unique Value Proposition, so I harp on answering, "Why Choose You?" as a place you have to be comfortable with going.

Q: Were you surprised by any of the statistics you found in your research? Did any of them meet your expectations?

A: The aha moment for me was realizing that 2012 was the year that half of us in the US started using our smartphones in new and exciting, disruptive, ways and the speed of the cellular networks finally clicked, too. Think of when you ordered your first Uber . . .

Q: What has been your most rewarding experience as a freelancer?

A: Helping others see their crazy bright future and go confidently into it.

Q: How has researching for this book changed the way you think about freelancing if at all?

A: Understanding how difficult it is for most people to have a marketing mindset in order to get chosen in the gig economy. To be a successful freelancer, it is not enough to be the best in a particular skill set. You must embrace the additional skill of getting the attention of those doing the choosing.

Q: You interviewed people with several different levels of experience in freelancing. Do you think it is important to spend some amount of time in traditional job roles before striking out on your own? Can you jump right into the gig economy like the story of Leo the CEO and hope to be as successful as he is?

A: It is important to embrace the idea of lifelong learning and matching the job opportunities to the skillset you have at the time. If you're not starting out in a traditional job role, how can you gain the experience to jump to the next level? In almost all cases it takes being generous with your time and up for some grunt work. In our token freelancer Emma's case, a future Fulbright scholar, she worked a party for me—literally serving food and cleaning up with a smile. Since I hire a lot of independents, I saw something in her that allowed me to offer her an opportunity at ohso! design. She did some grunt work, but she also eventually learned a lot about marketing, including running full-fledged email marketing campaigns and understanding UVP at a level that most people don't. Those skills allowed her to market her brilliance in a different way, and it's safe to say, she stopped working in food service.

You mentioned Leo. He didn't just "jump in" to the gig economy. He had a natural entrepreneurial mindset from when he was a kid, selling things to other kids. He gained skills along the way and didn't start out cold.

You may say, "Ah, the age old 'you need experience to be hired,' but how do I get experience?" There are a multitude of organizations that you can match your passion with—a local cause that you can lend a hand to. You can learn tremendous skills and give back! Maintain their website, learn how to do fundraising, put together a newsletter, event planning, etc!

About the Author

Recently featured in *Forbes*, *Fast Company*, and *Inc.* Magazine, Olga Mizrahi is an instructor for the Digital Marketing Program at the University of California, Irvine Continuing Education and the author of *Sell Local. Think Global*, which Seth Godin hails as ". . . a hands on, idea-packed book for business people in search of growth."

Olga Mizrahi is best known for discovering other's Unique Value Proposition and communicating it boldly through innovative and easy to learn marketing techniques honed over years of working with clients big and small—from Dole to the local pediatric clinic.

She is currently a national speaker and marketing expert on the gig economy; a local Southern California business owner; a blogger for entrepreneurs and freelancers at ChunkofChange.com; and a small business columnist for *The Long Beach Post*.

Olga's fresh views on the freelance economy, personal branding, and entrepreneurial Unique Value Proposition have also been featured at Airbnb's Open Conference, Investor's Business Daily, and the AMEX Small Business Open.

When not doing all the things, you can find Olga skiing, mountain biking, or paddleboarding in California.